CITYSPOTS
PORTO

WHAT'S IN YOUR GUIDEBOOK?

Independent authors Impartial up-to-date information from our travel experts who meticulously source local knowledge.

Experience Thomas Cook's 165 years in the travel industry and guidebook publishing enriches every word with expertise you can trust.

Travel know-how Contributions by thousands of staff around the globe, each one living and breathing travel.

Editors Travel-publishing professionals, pulling everything together to craft a perfect blend of words, pictures, maps and design.

You, the traveller We deliver a practical, no-nonsense approach to information, geared to how you really use it.

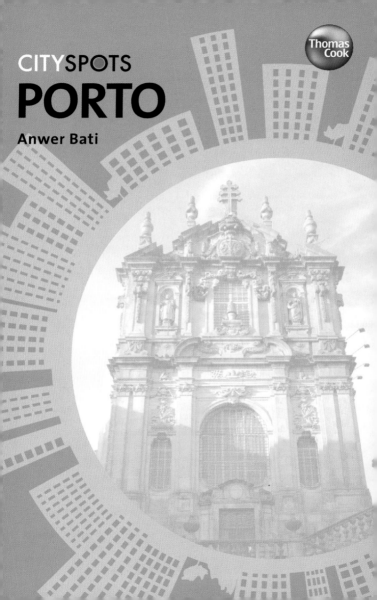

CITYSPOTS
PORTO

Anwer Bati

Thomas Cook

Written by Anwer Bati
Original photography by Anwer Bati
Front cover photography (Saint Ildefonso church) © Jon Arnold Images
Series design based on an original concept by Studio 183 Limited

Produced by Cambridge Publishing Management Ltd
Project Editor: Ross Hilton
Layout: Trevor Double
Maps: PC Graphics
Transport map: © Communicarta Limited

Published by Thomas Cook Publishing
A division of Thomas Cook Tour Operations Limited
Company Registration No. 1450464 England
PO Box 227, Unit 18, Coningsby Road
Peterborough PE3 8SB, United Kingdom
email: books@thomascook.com
www.thomascookpublishing.com
+ 44 (0) 1733 416477

ISBN: 978-1-84157-775-3

First edition © 2007 Thomas Cook Publishing
Text © 2007 Thomas Cook Publishing
Maps © 2007 Thomas Cook Publishing
Series/Project Editor: Kelly Anne Pipes
Production/DTP: Steven Collins

Printed and bound in Spain by GraphyCems

CONTENTS

SYMBOLS KEY

The following symbols are used throughout this book:

ⓐ address ☎ telephone ⓦ website address ⓔ email
🕙 opening times ⓝ public transport connections ❶ important

The following symbols are used on the maps:

ℹ️ information office		⭕	city
✈️ airport		⭕	large town
➕ hospital		◦	small town
🛡️ police station		═	motorway
🚊 railway station		—	main road
Ⓜ️ metro		—	minor road
✝️ cathedral		—	railway
❶ numbers denote featured cafés & restaurants			

Hotels and restaurants are graded by approximate price
as follows:

£ budget ££ mid-range £££ expensive

▶ *King Pedro IV surveys the Praça da Liberdade*

Introduction

Porto (also known as Oporto, but not locally) is – as the name suggests – a port, and capital of the Porto district in northwest Portugal. Built on the banks of the River Douro, it is the second largest city in the country, after Lisbon, and has always been the second in economic and commercial importance. Evidence of its history is easily seen today, but the main attraction is the remarkable, and fascinating, old town, south of the Praça de Liberdade, designated a UNESCO World Heritage Site in 1996.

The centre of Porto is built on the granite Penaventosa Hill, sloping down to the north bank of the Douro, which is spanned by six impressive bridges. The bustling Ribeira area, on the river – with its bars and restaurants – is a particular attraction. As is the city's architecture, dating from medieval times to cutting-edge modern. Porto is a lively place with several museums, a university, major performance venues and a new concert hall and opera house. The central part of the city is home to around 300,000 people, with many more in the sprawling suburbs.

One of the city's main industries is port wine – named after the city – which developed there, and for which the main market has traditionally been England, with many of the leading port houses originally owned by British firms.

Although it is a business city, Porto attracts many visitors. And its location on the Douro means that one of the most popular activities for visitors is to take a train or a cruise up the river valley, once they have explored the city itself. Visitors choose Porto for the architecture and culture (though there are relatively few formal sights), and to enjoy the city's atmosphere.

◔ The Cais da Ribeira, Porto's birthplace

When to go

SEASONS & CLIMATE

Porto is in the north of Portugal, summer average daytime temperatures hover around 21°C (70°F), though it can get as high as 25°C (77°F); however, it is mild for most of the year. The Atlantic climate also means that it can rain, sometimes heavily, during much of the year – particularly from October to April, although there is also plenty of sunshine. It's best to visit from June to September (especially July and August) if you want to avoid rain and make the most of the riverside cafés and the Douro itself. This, of course, is the most popular time for visitors, so late spring or early autumn are good options if you don't mind getting wet occasionally.

ANNUAL EVENTS

There are numerous festivals, events and performances during the year. The main annual events are listed below; for further information check ⓦ www.portoturismo.pt

February

Fantasporto Porto's main film festival, and one of the best known in Portugal – showing horror, thriller, fantasy, science fiction and cult movies. ⓦ www.fantasporto.online.pt

April

Fazar a Festa Theatre festival, with Portuguese and international companies performing outdoors and in tents.
ⓦ www.teatroartimagem.org

● *Porto's mild climate supports lush vegetation such as palm trees*

May

Children's Week A week of theatre shows and events aimed at children.

June

Feira do Livro (Book Fair) Going since 1920, and now held at the Rosa Mota Pavilion. ⓐ Rua Dom Manuel II ⓣ 225 430 360
Serralves em Festa Forty hours of exhibitions, music, dance and other free performances in Serralves park during the first weekend in June. ⓦ www.serralves.pt
Festa de São João (Feast of St John the Baptist) See page 14.

July

Jazz no Parque (Jazz in the Park) Held at Serralves park.
Encontros com o Barroco Baroque music concerts in churches.
Porto Cartoon World Festival A major cartoon event at the Museu Nacional de Impressa, and other venues.

August

Noites Ritual Rock Rock Festival, with Portuguese bands, at Palácio de Cristal.
Festas de S Bartholomeu (Feast of St Bartholomew) A colourful procession, among other celebrations.

September/October

Festival de Jazz do Porto High-quality international jazz festival held at Rivoli Teatro Municipal.
Sentidos Grátis A visual arts festival held in the streets.

December

Corrida de S Silvestre A running race, which takes place at night (when the city is decorated with Christmas lights).

Feira de Artesanato A fair promoting regional crafts, at the Palácio de Cristal. Ⓦ www.aarn.pt

PUBLIC HOLIDAYS

Portugal has rather a lot of public holidays, when all official buildings, many museums, most offices, and a few restaurants and bars are closed. Transport schedules are also affected. Note that 24 June is a holiday only in Porto and Braga, and not nationally.

New Year's Day (Ano Novo) 1 Jan
Day before Ash Wednesday (Entrudo/Cinzas Carnival) Feb/Mar
Good Friday (Sexta-feira Santa) Mar/Apr
Liberation Day (Liberadade) 25 Apr
Labour Day (Trabalhador) 1 May
Corpus Christi (Corpo de Deuslate) May/early June
National Day of Portugal (Dia de Portugal) 10 June
Porto Day (Festa de São João) 24 June
Assumption of the Virgin (Assunção da Nossa Senhora) 15 Aug
Republic Day (Implantação de República) 5 Oct
All Saints' Day (Todos os Santos) 1 Nov
Independence Day (Restauração de Independência) 1 Dec
Immaculate Conception (Imaculada Conceição) 8 Dec
Christmas Day (Natal) 25 Dec

Festa de São João

Although the festival celebrating the birth of St John the Baptist (patron saint of Porto) is officially on 24 June, around the time of the June solstice and the longest day of the year, the people of Porto (and the many visitors) start celebrating the night before. It's when the locals, famed for their reserve, let rip.

One of the more bizarre aspects of the festival is that revellers carry plastic hammers (you'll be given one at the tourist office) with which they amiably hit one another. Restaurants and bars are packed, and festivities carry on until the morning, with fireworks (the best place to watch them is Ribeira) at midnight. There are also open air music events around the city, and many parties.

On the feast day itself, things are somewhat more restrained, with church services and concerts. In the evening, the city centre has a colourful parade, Rusgas de São João, from Batalha to the Praça de Liberdade.

On the 25th, you can watch the famous, traditional and picturesque Rabelos Regatta on the Douro, starting at noon at Cabedelo. The wooden boats, *barcos rabelos*, are of the type that traditionally transported port barrels down the river. The boats are owned by the various port lodges, and bear their symbols – and some of the crews treat the competition remarkably seriously. The best place to see the race is from between the Arrábida bridge and the Luís I bridge, perhaps while having lunch along the river.

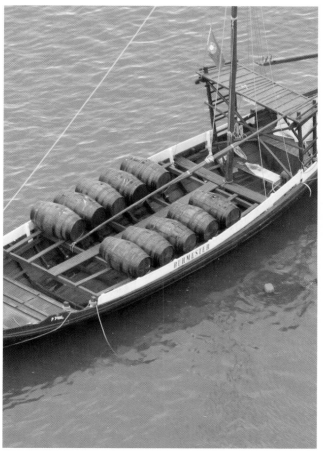

◔ Barcos rabelos, *the wooden boats on show during the Festa de São João*

History

Porto was originally founded as Cale, a Celtic trading settlement on the south bank of the Douro. In turn it was ruled by the Romans, who called it Portus Cale, the Visigoths and the Muslim Moors. Considerable conflict then followed between Muslims and Christians, and Porto – for a time capital of northern Portugal (Portucalense or Portucale – the origins of the country's name) – finally became Christian in 1092.

Three years later it was part of the lands of Henry of Burgundy. On the death of Ferdinand I, the last of Henry's descendants, his half-brother João (John I) founded the Portuguese royal house of Aviz. He married Philippa of Lancaster, daughter of John of Gaunt, and in 1386 Portugal and England became allies through the Treaty of Windsor.

By this time Porto had become a major port, and it was John's son Henry the Navigator, born in Porto in 1394, who made Portugal one of the greatest seafaring nations in the world, in the search for a route to the spices and other wealth of south Asia. This laid the foundation for the Portuguese empire, with colonies such as Brazil, Mozambique, Goa and Macao. Portugal (and Porto) became increasingly prosperous, reaching the height of wealth in the 17th and 18th centuries – by now ruled by the house of Bragança – after both gold and diamonds were discovered in Brazil.

The trade in port began in 1678, and was confirmed by the Methuen Treaty between Portugal and England in 1703. The production of port is one of the city's main industries to this day.

Napoleon's armies invaded in 1807, and occupied Porto, to be driven out by British forces under General Sir Arthur Wellesley (later the Duke of Wellington) in 1809. But Portuguese prosperity took a blow: the Portuguese royal family had fled to Brazil in the face of the French threat. It returned, but relinquished Brazil as a colony.

The monarchy fell in 1910, and Portugal became a republic, but was chaotically run until the rise of António Salazar in the 1930s. He was to rule, as dictator, until 1968 and an isolated Portugal languished during this period. A democratic revolution in 1974, and eventual entry to the European Community in 1986, led to the growth of economic prosperity once again, as well as a boom in tourism.

Porto has undergone major development, particularly after the 1996 UNESCO World Heritage listing, and its nomination as European Capital of Culture in 2001. As a result, many buildings have been restored, and its infrastructure improved – with a new metro system, improved local rail links and extensions to the tram system.

⬤ Azulejos *(hand-painted tiles) adorn many historic buildings*

Lifestyle

After decades of isolation, repression and economic stagnation, the people of Portugal have adapted well to democracy and modernity, and the freedom and prosperity these have brought them. But some traditional attitudes remain, particularly among older people and those in authority. Incomes are low by western European standards, but so are prices.

Despite its historical and economic importance, Porto's image, until recently, was quieter and less urbane than more sophisticated Lisbon, further south. Indeed, Porto has a reputation for being hard-working and somewhat conservative – the saying goes that 'Lisbon plays, Braga prays and Porto works'. But much has changed since the UNESCO and European Capital of Culture accolades, and the city now has a buzz to it and is a pretty relaxed place to visit. Hard-working northerners they may be, but the people – known for their dislike of authority – like to enjoy themselves, particularly when the weather is dry and sunny. And they like a good meal, and a decent amount of drink; however, drunkenness is very rare and strongly disapproved of. The locals have a certain reserve (though they are friendly), and tend to dress fairly formally. The best dress option for a visitor is smart casual, particularly when visiting churches (there is still a strong Catholic tradition in Portugal). The Portuenses (Porto natives) are proud of their country, their city and its history and visitors are expected to behave with decorum.

Porto has a substantial cultural life and a lively nightlife, particularly at weekends. And the biggest local passion is football, in particular FC Porto: European champions in 2004. When Portugal hosted the Euro 2004 championships, Porto's Dragão stadium was one of the main venues.

Given the importance of the port trade, developed by British merchants, and other historical links to England, Portugal's oldest ally, British people are not only frequent visitors, but are given a warm welcome. And English is widely spoken in hotels and restaurants.

◢ *The Majestic Café, a classic Porto establishment*

Culture

Although Porto has always been Portugal's second most important cultural centre, it has really taken off as a lively arts spot since its European Capital of Culture status in 2001. Several good museums offer art, artefacts and more unusual offerings, such as old trams. Port is also represented: you can visit the various shippers' lodges, and the recently opened Museu do Vinho do Porto.

Porto's architecture is another cultural attraction, and one of the reasons why part of the city is a UNESCO World Heritage Site. This is centred on the Ribeira district (the site also covers the Mosteiro da Serra do Pilar across the Douro, and the area around Sé cathedral), where the architecture dates from the Middle Ages to 19th-century neoclassical. Many fine churches in the centre of Porto display various architectural styles including medieval, Renaissance and baroque, and there are important neoclassical buildings such as S Bento railway station, the Palácio da Bolsa and the Hospital Santo Antonio. Look out for the many buildings decorated with *azulejos* (hand-painted tiles, usually with figurative designs) around the UNESCO area and the town centre. The Avenida da Boavista, and the area around it, has many impressive villas dating from the 19th century and the 1930s. Notable modern buildings in the city include the Museu de Arte Contemporânea (contemporary art museum), designed by Alvaro Siza Vieira in 1999, and Dutch architect Rem Koolhaas's Casa da Música, which opened in 2005.

Music, theatre and dance, both classical and contemporary, are very important in Porto, and Porto has a major orchestra, the

⬥ *The Museu do Vinho do Porto tells the story of port*

Orquestra Nacional do Porto. Movies too are also taken seriously, with several cinemas around town.

It's therefore well worth getting a Passe Porto (Porto Card), from a tourist office, which will give you free entry to municipal museums, unlimited use of public transport in the city, and discounts at other museums and attractions, including Douro cruises. Some shops and restaurants also offer discounts. A one-day walking card (no transport) is €3.50; one day with transport is €7.50; two days €11.50; and three days €15.50.

The six bridges (*pontes*) spanning the river aren't strictly cultural, but are well worth a mention. From east to west: Ponte do Freixo opened in 1995; Ponte São João (railway bridge; built in 1991) replaced the Ponte Maria Pia bridge, dating from 1877 – designed by Gustave Eiffel. Next is the concrete Ponte do Infante (road bridge); dominating the Ribeira quayside is Ponte Dom Luis I, designed on two levels by an associate of Eiffel, and opened in 1886. Finally, near the mouth of the Douro, is Ponte da Arrábida, the largest concrete bridge in the world when it opened in 1963.

● *Sandeman, a temple dedicated to that most famous of Porto exports*

Shopping

Porto is a major city, so there is no shortage of shopping, whether for local specialities or everyday items. And prices, apart from in international chains, are among the lowest you'll find in western Europe.

The main shopping street in central Porto is Rua de Santa Catarina, where there are mainly clothes and shoe shops (shoes are cheap in Portugal), including the Via Catarina shopping centre. Also check out the Rua Passos Manuel, nearby. Several other shopping centres are dotted around the city, including two (the Peninsula and the Cidade do Porto) near the Casa da Música in the Boavista area, and the Arrábida shopping centre (with cinemas and restaurants), on the Vila Nova de Gaia side of the Douro, near the Arrábida bridge. The Boavista area also has many upmarket designer shops.

But one of the main pleasures of shopping in Porto is in finding small food, wine and craft shops. And discovering them, simply by wandering around the centre of town, is one of the highlights of any trip to Porto. Look out for old books, ceramics (including Portugal's famous hand-painted tiles, *azulejos*), textiles and jewellery.

And don't forget the city's markets. The main one is the colourful semi-covered Bolhão food market, not far from Rua de Santa Catarina (the market is to be renovated during 2007). The streets around it also have a number of tempting food shops, from where you can put together a picnic. Local specialities to go for include sausages, charcuterie, cheese, pastries and salt cod. Other markets include the Feira des Antiguidades e

🔺 *Wonderfully ornate delicatessen*

Velharias, an antiques market at the Praça Dr Sá Cameiro on the third Saturday of each month, and the flower market, Feira das Flores (ⓐ Praça da Liberdade ◷ 08.00–17.00 Sun Apr–Oct).

There are several shops around town selling port and Douro wines. You can also buy port at the various lodges in Vila Nova de Gaia, and at the airport.

Some of the museums, particularly the Museu de Arte Contemporânea, also have good shops.

USEFUL SHOPPING PHRASES

What time do the shops open/close?
A que horas abrem/fecham as lojas?
A kee orah abrayng/fayshown ash lohzhash?

How much is this?
Quanto custa isto?
Kwantoo kooshta eeshtoo?

Can I try this on?
Posso provar este?
Possoo proovahr aysht?

My size is ...
O meu tamanho (número) é ...
Oo mayo tamanyo (noomiroo) eh ...

I'll take this one, thank you
Levo este, obrigado
Lehvoo aysht, ohbreegahdoo

This is too large/too small/too expensive.
Do you have any others?
Este é muito grande/muito pequeno/muito caro. Tem outros?
Aysht eh muingtoo grangdi/muingtoo pikaynoo/muingtoo kahroo. Tayng ohtroosh?

Eating & drinking

Portuguese cuisine can't be called sophisticated – what you will find in most restaurants amounts to versions of home or country cooking, often using fresh herbs and spices – but the food is much better than in southern Portugal and portions are extremely generous (you can ask for a *meia dose*, or half-portion). Note, however, that you will be charged for what might appear to be freebies plonked on your table, such as bread, olives and charcuterie. If you don't want them, send them back, or simply don't eat them. But eating out is relatively cheap in Portugal.

Fish and seafood are a mainstay, including the ubiquitous *bacalhau* (dried salt cod), which supposedly has enough recipes for every day of the year.

Meat is just as popular: game, beef and goat, and in particular pork: spit-roasted suckling pig is a favourite. And offal is widespread on menus. Porto specialises in stewed tripe, cooked with haricot beans. Indeed the nickname for the locals is *tripeiros* ('tripe eaters'), supposedly because available meat was given to sailors, leaving only tripe to eat in the city. Portuguese menus often feature soups, including the filling bread soups, *açordas*. Brazilian dishes, and a number of Brazilian restaurants,

PRICE RATING
The restaurant price guides given in this book indicate the approximate cost of a three-course dinner without drinks.
£ €15 or under   ££ €15–€50   £££ Over €50

also feature. Portuguese desserts are very sweet, and are often egg-based.

The Portuguese tend to have a very light breakfast, but a much fuller lunch and dinner. Restaurants (*restaurantes*) normally open from 12.00–15.00 and 19.00–22.00. But the lifestyle of the Portuenses is changing, and later opening hours are starting to reflect this, particularly in tourist areas. Other eateries include *toscas* – cheap family-run affairs with hearty food; *tabernas,* where you eat at a shared table; *cervejarias* serve

● *Fresh fish forms the basis of the local cuisine*

beer and snacks; a *casa de pasto* is a dining room serving a cheap three-course meal at lunchtimes; *marisqueiras* serve fish and seafood; and *churrasqueiras* serve grilled meat.

Many restaurants include a service charge, but simpler places might not – in which case leave a 10 per cent tip. Smoking is currently permitted in bars and restaurants, but like other European cities, pressure is mounting to ban it.

You should have no difficulty finding tasty snacks, cakes, pastries and sandwiches of all kinds, including tapas, borrowed from Spain (sometimes also called *petiscos*). There are markets, of course, with cheese, charcuterie, bread, fruit and vegetables to buy – and several pleasant places to have a picnic. In winter, there are roast chestnut stalls around the city.

Portugal is one of the biggest wine producers and consumers (per head) in Europe. Portuguese wines are made with indigenous grape varieties, and are of a high standard, particularly those designated DOC, although house wines (*vinho da casa*) are good value and perfectly drinkable. Local Douro wines, such as white Planalto, are very pleasing. Vinho Verde is young, very dry and slightly fizzy – both whites and (normally weaker) reds.

The best-known wine from the area though is port, which includes: Ruby (young and fruity, and the cheapest), Tawny (aged in wood), Vintage (aged for years in bottles, and the most expensive), Coiheita (Tawny from a single year), and white port, normally drunk as an aperitif. Madeira is a fortified wine from the Portuguese-ruled Atlantic island of the same name. The best-known Portuguese spirit is *aguardente* – made from different fruits.

USEFUL DINING PHRASES

I would like a table for ... people
Queria uma mesa para ... pessoas
Kireea ooma mehza para ... pesoash

May I have the bill, please?
Pode-me dar a conta, por favor?
Pohd-mi dahr er kohngta, poor favohr?

Waiter/waitress!
Faz favor!
Fash favohr!

Could I have it well cooked/medium/rare, please?
Posso escolher bem passado/médio/mal passado, por favor?
Possoo ishkoolyer bayng pasahdoo/mahl pasahdoo, poor favohr?

I am a vegetarian. Does this contain meat?
Sou vegetariano. Isto tem carne?
Soh vezhetahreeahnoo. Ishtoo tehng kahrni?

Where is the toilet (restroom) please?
Por favor, onde são os lavabos?
Poor favohr, ohngdee sowng oos lavahboosh?

I would like a cup of/two cups of/another coffee/tea
Queria uma chávena de/duas chávenas de/outro café/chá
Kireea ooma shahvna di/dooash shahvnash di ohtroo kafeh/shah

Entertainment & nightlife

Porto has a lively nightlife, particularly at weekends in summer. For a start, many of the main sights, such as the cathedral, the Luis I bridge and the Clérigos Tower, are illuminated at night, so simply walking around is something to look forward to.

Plenty of bars and cafés allow for a late drink after dinner (when you can sit outside on Ribeira quay or at the mouth of the Douro and enjoy the river view in good weather), and a decent selection of clubs and discos around town delay bedtime. The Foz do Douro area is the most happening place to head for in summer, particularly the Avenida do Brasil. And the last three or four years have seen a range of new bars and restaurants, many glass-fronted, and with roof terraces opening up on the quayside at Vila Nova de Gaia.

Theatre performances are in Portuguese, of course, but there are also many musical and dance performances to go to, where language isn't a barrier, sometimes with major international artists performing, at venues such as the Teatro Nacional de São João, the Rivoli Teatro Municipal, the Coliseu do Porto and the new Casa da Música.

There are also several music festivals during the year, including the Jazz Festival (centred on the Rivoli theatre), the outdoor Jazz no Parque on the old tennis court of Serralves park and Noites do Palácio and Noites Ritual Rock, both at the Palácio de Cristal. Major rock performances are most likely to be at the Coliseu, dating from the 1940s, which also stages opera and other spectacles (ⓐ Rua de Passos Manuel 137 ⓣ 223 394 940 ⓦ www.coliseudoporto.pt ⓝ Metro: line D, S Bento or Line A, B, C, E Bolhão).

● *There is no shortage of bars in Porto*

If you want to catch a movie, there are a number of cinemas in central Porto, mostly showing films in their original language – including English – with Portuguese subtitles. In particular the Cinema Batalha, opened in 1947 and recently renovated, which has two bars and a terrace (🕐 until 02.00 during the week, and 04.00 at weekends), as well as a restaurant (🕐 12.00–15.00, 20.00–22.30) and a coffee shop (🅰 Praça de Batalha 47 📞 222 011 913 🌐 www.cinemabatalha.com Ⓝ Metro: line D, S Bento).

There is a multiscreen cinema in the Cidade do Porto shopping centre in Boavista (🅰 Centro Commerical Cidade do Porto, Rua Gonçalo Sampaio 350 📞 226 009 164 Ⓝ Metro: line A, B, C, E Casa da Música).

You will find events listings in the free monthly *cultura.norte*, and the quarterly *Agenda do Porto* (in Portuguese and English 🌐 www.agendadoporto.pt): both available from tourist offices and hotels; and on the local tourist website 🌐 www.portoturismo.pt

Sport & relaxation

SPECTATOR SPORTS
Football
You can share the local obsession with football by watching
FC Porto (🅐 Estádio do Dragão 🕿 225 570 400
🌐 www.fcporto.pt (in Portuguese and English) Ⓜ Metro: lines
A, B, C, E Estádio do Dragão), or Porto's less well-known football
club, **Boavista FC** (🅐 Estádio do Bessa, Rua 1° de Janeiro 🕿 226
071 004/5 🌐 www.boavistafc.pt Ⓜ Metro: lines A, B, C, E Casa
da Música).

PARTICIPATION SPORTS
Activities
Vigorous and challenging activities, including riding, can be
booked through **Arrepio-Animação** (🅐 Rua Prof Antão Almeida
Garret 229 🕿 228 303 940). Tennis courts include **Lawn Ténis da
Foz** (🅐 Rua João Martins Branco 154 🕿 226 180 933) and **Oporto
Cricket and Lawn Tennis Club** (🅐 Rua do Campo Alegre 532
🕿 226 091 719). To find a **gym**, consult the tourist office website
(🌐 www.portoturismo.pt) or your nearest tourist office.

Boat and bus trips
There are all sorts of boat trips along the Douro, in either simple
rabelos or more lavish craft, many with English-speaking guides.
The best central point of information and to book is Porto Tours
(by the cathedral), where you can also book bus tours both in or
out of the city. For hop-on, hop-off open-top double-decker
guided bus tours of the city (🕿 808 200 166).

Porto Tours ⓐ Torre Medieval, Calçada D Pedro Pitões 15
ⓣ call centre 222 000 073 ⓦ www.portotours.com

Golf
Quinta da Barca, 30 km (19 miles) from Porto. ⓐ Barca do Lago
ⓣ 253 966 723 ⓔ quintabarca@clix.pt

● *There's no better way to see the city than a cruise down the Douro*

Estela, 35 km (22 miles) away. ⓐ Rio Alto ⓣ 252 601 567
ⓦ www.estelagolfe.pt

Watersports

Don't swim in the sea anywhere near the centre of Porto. Go to
the **Clube Fluvial Portuense** instead (ⓐ Rua Aleixo Mota ⓣ 226
198 460 ⓔ clubefluvialportuense@clix.pt ⓛ 08.00–22.00
Mon–Fri, 09.00–18.00 Sat, 09.00–13.00 Sun (summer);
08.00–21.00 Mon–Fri, 09.00–18.00 Sat, 09.00–13.00 Sun
(winter) ⓝ Bus: 207 to Pasteleira).

You can learn to surf at **Surfing Life Clube Matosinhos**
(ⓐ Praça Cidade S Salvador 295 ⓣ 91 756 7092
ⓦ www.surfinglifeclub.com) or **Escola de Surf do Norte**
(ⓐ Praia de Matosinhos ⓣ 229 379 665/96 315 6441
ⓦ www.clubedesportoaventura.web.pt).

Accommodation

Porto has all types of accommodation, though much of it is outside the UNESCO World Heritage area. Note that central hotel accommodation is in short supply during the city's many business events and in summer; however, outside summer, it is often easier to get a room at weekends than during the week. Always make sure you book well in advance.

Unless you have booked an inclusive package, it pays to investigate thoroughly on the web. The Porto tourist website (ⓦ www.portoturismo.pt) carries a comprehensive list of hotels and their facilities, and provides links to the hotels' own websites. The recommendations below are only a few of the good hotels to choose from. The ratings indicate the average price per double room per night. Some rooms, particularly those with views, may be more expensive than the ratings suggest, others might be cheaper. Many hotels include a buffet breakfast in their rates, others charge a supplement.

HOTELS

Hotel Boa Vista £ A late-19th-century hotel at the mouth of the Douro, with modernised rooms (the most expensive with a sea view) and a rooftop swimming pool. Not far from Serralves park.

PRICE RATING
The ratings below indicate the approximate cost of a double room, usually including breakfast, per night.
£ under €100   ££ €100–€150   £££ upwards of €150

Esplanada do Castelo 58 225 320 020
www.hotelboavista.com Bus: line 200, Mercado do Foz

Hotel São José £ Small, family-run traditional hotel in the city centre, close to the World Heritage area. Rua da Alegria 172 222 080 261 www.hotelsaojose.pa-net.pt Metro: lines A, B, C, E Bolhão

Residencial dos Aliados £ A good, simple, central budget choice in an art nouveau building. Some rooms can be noisy. Rua Eliseo de Melo 27 222 004 853 www.residencialaliados.com Metro: line D, Aliados

Eurostars Hotel Das Artes £–££ Very good value 4-star hotel, just by the Museu Soares Dos Reis, and close to the Palácio de Cristal. A good location for most of Porto's sights. Rua do Rosário 160–164 222 071 250 www.eurostarsdasartes.com Bus: 3, 6, 20, 24, 35, 37, 52, 78

Hotel da Bolsa £–££ Close to the old stock exchange building, convenient for exploring the Ribeira area. Built on the site of an old monastery, it has an impressive 19th-century façade; the rooms, however, are functional and modern, with the best having a view of the river. Rua Ferreira Borges 101 222 026 768 www.hotelbolsa.com Metro: line D, S Bento

Grande Hotel do Porto ££ Porto's oldest existing hotel, dating from 1880, is situated right in the heart of the main shopping area. The rooms, last refurbished in 2002, are modern, but the

🔺 Hotel Dom Henrique offers great views over the city

public areas, including the good restaurant, retain their period charm. ⓐ Rua de Santa Catarina 197 ❶ 222 076 690 ⓦ www.grandehotelporto.com Ⓝ Metro: lines A, B, C, E Bolhão

Hotel Fénix Porto ££ A modern hotel, officially 4-star, but with reasonable prices. Situated near the Rotunda de Boavista, and the Casa da Música. ⓐ Rua Gonçalo Sampaio 282 ❶ 226 071 800 ⓦ www.fenixporto.com Ⓝ Metro: lines A, B, C, E, Casa da Música

Hotel Mercure Batalha ££ Very well placed for both the city centre and Ribeira, this comfortable hotel by Porto's main theatre is a good choice. ⓐ Praça da Batalha 116 ❶ 222 043 300 ⓦ www.mercure.com Ⓝ Metro: line D, S Bento

Hotel Dom Henrique ££–£££ Basically a business hotel, but with good rooms and facilities, and great views from the bar on the 17th floor. A convenient location for central Porto. ⓐ Rua Guedes Azevedo 179 ❶ 223 401 616 ⓦ www.hoteldomhenrique.pt Ⓝ Metro: lines A, B, C, D, E Trindade

Pestana Porto ££–£££ By the Douro in the Ribeira area with fine views of the river from the best of the well-appointed rooms. ⓐ Praça da Ribeira 1 ❶ 223 402 300 ⓦ www.llhotels.com/pestanoporto Ⓝ Metro: line D, S Bento (a 15-minute walk)

Infante de Sagres £££ One of Porto's most luxurious hotels, full of character if a little old-fashioned, with plush public areas furnished with antiques, a good (and reasonably priced)

restaurant and a cosy bar. Well located for the UNESCO area.
ⓐ Praça Filipa de Lencastre 62 ⓣ 223 398 500
ⓦ www.hotelinfantesagres.pt ⓝ Metro: line D, Aliados

Sheraton Porto Hotel & Spa £££ Opened in 2003, this glitzy
luxury hotel, on 12 floors – with a spa and pool – is the best in
town, with a lively bar, a good restaurant and state-of-the-art
rooms offering considerable comfort. Because it is in Boavista
rather than the city centre, prices are lower than they are in
some less good central hotels. The buffet breakfast is excellent.
ⓐ Rua Tenente Valadim 146 ⓣ 220 404 000
ⓦ www.sheraton.com/porto ⓝ Metro: lines A, B, C, E Francos

YOUTH HOSTELS
Pousada da Juventude do Porto Porto's excellent youth hostel
has a view of the mouth of the Douro, a bar, a kitchen, internet
access and parking. There are several types of accommodation,
but make sure you book in advance. ⓐ Rua Paulo da Gama 551
ⓣ 226 177 257 ⓦ www.movijovem.pt ⓝ Bus: 207 to Pasteleira

CAMPSITES
Campismo Prelada The city's main campsite is some distance to
the northwest of the city centre, but is easily accessible by bus.
ⓐ Rua do Monte dos Burgos ⓣ 228 312 616 ⓝ Bus: 300 to
Campismo Prelada

THE BEST OF PORTO

Porto doesn't have a huge number of formal sights or attractions, and those it does have are mainly in walking distance of each other, or a short metro or taxi ride away. You'll get as much from relaxing and enjoying the lifestyle and atmosphere as in trying to pack in as much as possible.

TOP 10 ATTRACTIONS

- **Cais da Ribeira (Ribeira Quay)** The Ribeira quayside, a pleasure to walk along and where you will find some of the town's liveliest bars and restaurants (see page 61).

- **Torre dos Clérigos (Clérigos Tower)** Climbing up the tower will reward you with incomparable views of the town centre and the World Heritage area (see page 66).

- **Fundação de Serralves Museu de Arte Contemporânea (Serralves Foundation Museum of Contemporary Art)** A few hours spent at the Museum and in the park will be one of the highlights of your trip (see page 94).

- **Sé Catedral** Porto's most important building, and a major landmark (see page 71).

- **Palácio da Bolsa (Stock Exchange Palace)** A guided tour around the grand interior of the neoclassical former stock exchange is well worthwhile (see page 66).

- **Igreja de São Franciso (Church of St Francis)** In a city full of impressive churches, the rococo interior of this one is perhaps the most outstanding (see page 65).

- **Festa de São João (Feast of St John the Baptist)** If you're in town during the festival (24 June), you'll see the Portuenses at their most lively (see page 14).

- **Visit to a port lodge** It would be a shame to visit Porto and not visit one of the port lodges to have a tasting (see page 68).

- **A walk along one of the Douro bridges** Walking along any of the central bridges will give you superb views (see page 22).

- **A cruise down the Douro Valley** Cruises can be as short as an hour, or much, much longer. A train ride up the valley is equally picturesque (see page 36).

Ornate windows typical of Ribeira

HALF-DAY: PORTO IN A HURRY
You'll have time to see just the World Heritage Site area, including a visit to the Clérigos Tower, the cathedral and the Ribeira district.

1 DAY: TIME TO SEE A LITTLE MORE
Now you can also walk across the Luis I bridge to visit the Mosteiro de Serra, see more of central Porto and have time to pop into a museum, such as the Museu Nacional Soares Dos Reis, or a church or two. You might also have time for some shopping in the Rua de Santa Catarina.

2–3 DAYS: SHORT CITY-BREAK
Now you can really get to know Porto. You shouldn't miss the Museu de Arte Contemporânea and Serralves park, and go to the nearby Boavista area to see the villas of the wealthy and the Casa da Música. You should also have time to visit the Museu do Carro Eléctrico (Tram Museum), and the nearby Palácio Cristal park, the Museu Romântico and maybe the Museu do Vinho do Porto. Also visit the Palácio da Bolsa and the neighbouring Casa do Infante. If you can, also try to visit the Gaia district and its port lodges.

LONGER: ENJOYING PORTO TO THE FULL
If you're in Porto for longer, you can really relax, enjoy a few long lunches, see a bit of the newer parts of the city, visit the Foz area and the mouth of the Douro, and perhaps take a cruise or boat trip up the the Douro Valley, or visit attractive towns (around an hour away) such as Guimarães and Braga.

● *Don't miss the medieval streets of the World Heritage area*

Something for nothing

Walking around is the cheapest – and one of the most rewarding – things you can do in Porto. You'll mostly be walking anyway, around the city centre and Ribeira, admiring the architecture, but you should also cross the Luis I bridge (from which you will get great views) to Vila Nova de Gaia, where most of the port lodges, such as Graham's, are free to visit. You can also walk along the Douro to the mouth of the river, and the attractive seaside area. Boavista is also another appealing area to walk in, stopping to admire the new Casa da Música, from the centre of town to the sea along the Avenida da Boavista.

Porto's many churches, including the cathedral, are also free, as are parks such as the Palácio Cristal, the Parque da Cidade and many other green spaces around town. Some museums and sights, such as Casa Tait, are also free; others, such as the Museu Romântico, are free at weekends; and the Soares Dos Reis museum is free on Sunday mornings and public holidays. And, although Porto is cheaper than most European cities, window shopping or a visit to the Bolhão, one of the other markets, or a tempting food shop, needn't cost a penny.

Then there are Porto's main festivals, many of which, such as Serralves em Festa during the first weekend of June (🕐 08.00 Sat–24.00 Sun 🌐 www.serralves.pt), offer free events. And to take part in the exuberant Festa de São João (see page 14) doesn't have to cost you anything extra. Visiting the Porto Book Fair in June (see page 11) is also free.

If you buy a Passe Porto (Porto Card; see page 55), of course, all the municipal museums and local public transport are free, plus you'll get substantial discounts at other attractions.

⬤ *The sublime exterior of the São Nicalau church – free to all*

When it rains

It can rain rather a lot in Porto, particularly in winter, and showers can be pretty persistent. But that shouldn't stop you from enjoying yourself, although walking on the cobbled streets of the old city, or on the slippery pavements of the city centre, can be rather hazardous – make sure you take suitable shoes.

The metro system is, however, clean, new and efficient, so it's a good option for getting around, as are the reasonably priced taxis which you will find at ranks around town. So you can stay dry when making your way to one of the city's smaller museums which you might not have thought of going to on a sunny day; or to one of Porto's churches. A ride in one of Porto's ancient trams is a fun option. And a warming port tasting at one of the shippers' lodges, as well as a tour, might be just the thing to go for.

Otherwise, the most enjoyable way to escape the rain is to pop into a café for a drink, or to go to a restaurant and have a lengthy lunch, maybe trying out some of the more unusual local specialities. Most restaurants on the Ribeira quayside have umbrellas outside, so there's no need to retreat indoors. And some of the cafés along both sides of the Douro are glass-fronted, so you can still enjoy a view of the river. Porto also has several shopping centres, most with cafés, so you could always do a bit of shopping while you wait for the rain to subside.

Since most films shown in Portugal are in their original language, with subtitles, you should easily be able to find an English-language film to watch if you really can't face the rain.

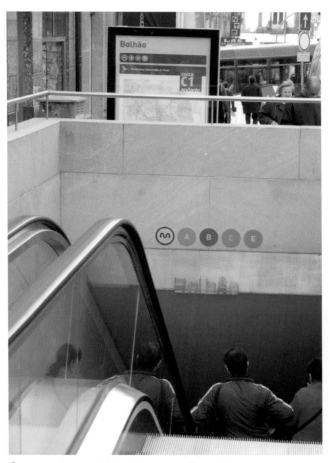

⬥ *Going underground – keep dry between sights with the metro*

On arrival

TIME DIFFERENCES

Portugal follows Greenwich Mean Time (GMT): from the end of March to the end of October, the clocks are put ahead 1 hour. In the Portuguese summer, at 12.00, the time elsewhere is:

Australia Eastern Standard Time 21.00, Central Standard Time 20.30, Western Standard Time 19.00

Britain 12.00

New Zealand 23.00

South Africa 13.00

USA and Canada Newfoundland Time 08.30, Atlantic Canada Time 08.00, Eastern Time 07.00, Central Time 06.00, Mountain Time 05.00, Pacific Time 04.00, Alaska 03.00.

ARRIVING

By air

Francisco Sá Carneiro airport is 15 km (9 miles) northwest of Porto's city centre. Note that, although the airport is state-of-the-art, you might have to walk some distance to get to the baggage hall. Arrivals are on the ground floor: café, newsagent and ATM machine to the left, car hire firms to the right; with a state tourist office in the concourse.

It takes around 30–35 minutes to get in to central Porto by car or taxi. The metro (line E) takes about the same time and runs every 25 minutes.

Aeroporto Francisco Sá Carneiro ① 229 432 400 ⓦ www.ana-aeroportos.pt

By train

Long-distance trains arrive at Campanhã station to the east of Porto. Take a metro or taxi to your hotel, or get a local train to São Bento railway station in the city centre (about ten minutes), and then take a metro or taxi.

Campanhã ⓐ Largo da Estação de Campanhã ❶ 225 191 374/808 208 200 (07.00–23.00)

São Bento ⓐ Praça Almeida Garrett ❶ 222 051 714/808 208 208 (07.00–23.00)

CP (Portuguese Railways) ⓦ www.cp.pt

By car

If coming from the north, you are likely to be arriving on the IC1 or the A3/IP1; for the city centre, follow signs to Aliados or Centro – the city centre can get very congested and beware the complex one-way systems. Car parks include: ⓐ Rua Fernandes Tomás, ⓐ Avenida da Boavista, ⓐ Rua de Cervantes and ⓐ Rua de Cedofeita.

🔺 *Checking in at Francisco Sá Carneiro airport*

FINDING YOUR FEET

The pace of life in Porto isn't very different to back home. And with the help of a map you should have no difficulty in finding your way around; everything is well signposted, and many locals speak at least a little English and will be helpful.

Comfortable shoes with non-slip soles are a good idea, to cope with steep cobbled streets and slippery pavements when it rains.

Portuguese can be difficult for foreigners to pronounce. A good idea is to write your destination down, to give to a taxi driver or ticket office for example.

ORIENTATION

The heart of the city centre is Praça de Liberdade and the Avenida dos Aliados, dominated at the northern end by the Câmara Municipal (Town Hall), which is illuminated at night. The Boavista area, and Serralves park, are some way to the west. To the south is the old town, the Ribeira area and the Douro. Across the river from Ribeira is Vila Nova de Gaia. The cathedral, and neighbouring Paço Episcopa (bishop's palace), are key landmarks to orientate yourself – as is the Torre dos Clérigos (Clérigos Tower), which can be seen from much of the city. S Bento station is another helpful landmark. And the Douro will almost certainly be downhill from you.

GETTING AROUND

Porto is well served by public transport, although many of the sights are within walking distance of one another. The best way to get round is by metro (● 06.00–01.00), which is clean, comfortable and efficient; the stations are rather discreetly marked. The extensive bus system (🕐 06.00–21.00) also has a network of night buses. (Bus numbers may change, as Porto's transport system develops.) Bus and metro ticket prices are modest. You can buy metro tickets from machines at the stops, and bus tickets on board or at the STCP bus company's offices and at tobacconists. They are cheaper if you buy them in advance. Don't forget to validate your ticket when you board a bus, by inserting it in the machine by the driver.

A one or three day Euro pass (€4 and €9) allows unlimited travel on buses, metros and trams (and is included with the Passe Porto (Porto Card). Note that passes also have to be validated.

IF YOU GET LOST, TRY ...

Excuse me, do you speak English?
Desculpe, fala Inglês?
Dishkoolp, fahla eenglays?

Excuse me, is this the right way to ... the cathedral/the tourist office/the castle/the old town?
Desculpe é este o caminho certo para ... a catedral/os serviços de informações turísticas (o turismo)/o castelo/a cidade velha?
Dishkoolp, eh aysht oo kameenyo sehrtoo para ... er katidrahl/oos sirveessoos de eemfoormasoyesh tooreehshteekash (oo tooreesmoo)/oo kastehloo/er seedahd vehlya?

Can you point to it on my map?
Pode indicá-lo no meu mapa?
Pohd eendeecahloo noo mayo mahpa?

Bus Route 500 stops
1. Lóios (destination on front of bus São Bento)
2. Estação S. Bento
3. Merc. Ferr. Borges
4. Ribeira (Infante)
5. Miragaia
6. Alfândega
7. Museu Vinho Porto
8. Museu C. Eléctrico
9. Bicalho
10. Ponte da Arrábida
11. Sécil
12. Gás
13. Cordoaria Velha
14. Fluvial
15. D. Leonor
16. Cantareira
17. Pilotos
18. Igreja da Foz
19. Castelo da Foz

Tram Route 1 stops
1. No name shown
2. Alfândega
3. Massarelos

Tram Route 18 stops
1. Carmo
2. Hosp. Sto. António
3. No Name shown
4. Massarelos

Tram Route 18 stops
1. Massarelos
2. Bicalho
3. Ponte da Arrábida
4. Sécil
5. Gás
6. Fluvial
7. Sobreiras
8. Cantareira

Metro	Historic Tram	Mainline Railway
A	1	
B	18	
C	18	
D		
E	Bus	
	500	

Bus & Tram stops

Our unique transport map includes the very new and highly efficient metro together with the historic tram routes and selected bus route 500. We have included bus route 500 since this will take you directly from the city centre to the Port Wine Museum. Not only that but it is a pleasant route out to the Atlantic coast which makes for a refreshing interlude from city life. The tram route 18 is supposedly going to be extended into the city centre along newly re-laid tracks. We haven't included this extension since it is unclear as to when this is to take place.

A Communicarta
Style 45 design
© Communicarta Ltd 2006 UDN.1
Map user Ref: WZFG/CS/OPO/2006/65/4

Hospital São João D

IPO

Pólo Universitário

Guimarães & Braga

Francos

Casa da Música

Salgueiros

Carolina Michaelis

Combatentes

Lapa

C B E A
Estádio do Dragão

Marquês

Faria Guimarães

Campanhã

Trindade

Bolhão

Aliados

Heroísmo

São Bento

Campo 24 de Agosto

São Bento

CP

Jardim do Morro

General Torres

Câmara Gaia

João de Deus D

Research and design by Robin Woods

There are currently two tram routes, though the system is being extended at the time of writing. The venerable vehicles (running 09.30–19.00) are an attraction in themselves. A funicular runs from Rua Augusto Rosa to the riverfront beneath the Luis I bridge.

Metro ⓦ www.metro-porto.pt

Buses and trams (in Porto) ⓦ www.stcp.pt

To get out of town, Porto has no central bus station. Consult one of the tourist offices (see page 137) for details. However, the local train system is pleasant, punctual and generally the best way to travel to nearby towns. Fares are low; buy tickets either at counters or from machines. You can catch local trains at either S Bento or Campanã stations.

There are taxi ranks in Porto's main squares, at S Bento station and at several other locations. Taxi fares are moderate and metered (expect to pay about €5 for a journey in the city centre). Your hotel and restaurants will also call taxis for you.

CAR HIRE

Portugal has fairly low car hire rates, but check whether it's cheaper to book your car with your plane or train ticket. However, you should need to hire a car (minimum age 23) only if you want to travel outside Porto.

A A Castanheira Budget Lda ⓐ Avenida da Boavista 918 ⓣ 226 065 256 ⓦ www.budget.pt

Auto Jardim ⓐ Rua Guerra Junqueiro 634 ⓣ 226 053 197 ⓦ www.auto-jardim.com

---

⚫ *The colourful houses and restaurants of the Cais da Ribeira*

The World Heritage area & Vila Nova de Gaia

Porto started lobbying for UNESCO World Heritage status in 1993, and the distinction was awarded in 1996. The classified area is essentially the medieval borough located within the 14th-century city wall, parts of which still exist. It includes the oldest buildings in Porto, and newer ones such as the old stock exchange and the Luis I bridge. It starts just south of the city's main square, Praça da Liberdade, and encompasses the Ribeira area, down to the Douro. It also stretches across the river to Vila Nova de Gaia, to include the Mosteiro da Serra do Pilar. The narrow cobbled streets of old houses wind down the steep hill, and can seem run-down at first – with washing hung out to dry, and buildings not in the best state of repair – before you take in the vibrant colours of the houses, and the lively bars and restaurants of Cais da Ribeira. Many buildings are rent-controlled, so landlords have had little incentive to keep them in good repair. However, all that is changing as the area becomes somewhat gentrified, and the city is slowly restoring it. But the sense of community is still palpable. Walking is really the only option, given the steep, narrow streets with limited bus services. There is only one metro station (S Bento), although taxis are an option.

Vila Nova de Gaia (known simply as Gaia locally) is technically a separate municipality to Porto proper. But no trip to Porto is complete without a visit to the monastery and port wine lodges, as well as the many quayside restaurants and bars.

SIGHTS & ATTRACTIONS

The main attraction is simply wandering around, as you head past a range of fascinating buildings from different periods down to the Douro for eating, drinking and cruising options.

Cais da Ribeira (Ribeira Quay)

The colourful quayside and the streets behind it were the site of Porto's origins, and once the hub of the city's seafaring and commercial activities, but the wealthy merchants who flourished there gradually moved out to live higher up the hill. By the end of the 19th century, the area was already in decline, but now it bustles with tourists instead. The restaurants are on the quayside itself, often within ancient arches. To the west of the

● *Classic Ribeira façade*

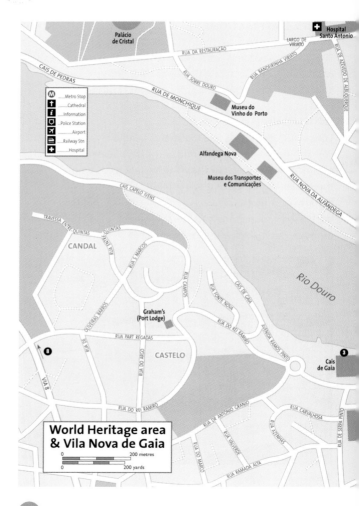

Palácio
de Cristal

Hospital
Santo António

LARGO DE
VIRIATO

RUA DA RESTAURAÇÃO

RUA DE ATEVEDO DE ALBUQUERQUE

RUA BANDEIRINHA VIRIATO

CAIS DE PEDRAS

RUA SOBRE DOURO

RUA DE MONCHIQUE

Museu do
Vinho do Porto

Ⓜ	Metro Stop
✝	Cathedral
ⓘ	Information
◉	Police Station
✈	Airport
🚆	Railway Stn
✚	Hospital

Alfandega Nova

Museu dos Transportes
e Comunicações

RUA NOVA DA ALFANDEGA

CAIS CAPELO IVENS

TRAVESSA ENTRE QUINTAS

Rio Douro

QUINTAS

CANDAL

RUA S. MARCOS

RUA CAMPOS

RUA PONTE NOVA

CAIS DE CAIA

AVENIDA RAMOS PINTO

OLIVEIRAS BAIXOS

Graham's
(Port Lodge)

RUA PART REGADAS

RUA DO REI RAMIRO

PONTE NOVA

CASTELO

Cais
de Gaia

VIA 8

RUA DO REI RAMIRO

RUA DE ANTÓNIO CRANJO

RUA CARVALHOSA

RUA AZENHAS

QUINA NIRES DO VIA

RUA DO MARCO

RUA VALVERDE

RUA RAMADA ALTA

World Heritage area
& Vila Nova de Gaia

0 ————— 200 metres

0 ————— 200 yards

quay is the small square, Praça da Ribeira, originally medieval, but much of it dating from the neoclassical period. To the east is spectacular Ponte Dom Luis I, with a span of 172 m (564 ft) built in 1886. The metro now runs on the upper level of this road bridge. From here there are unbeatable views of the Douro and its bridges, Ribeira and Gaia. In the streets behind the waterfront, look out for a 14th-century house in Rua de D Hugo, the 13th-century building in Rua de Baixo (No 5) and No 59 Rua de Reboleira, which almost certainly dates from the 14th century.

🅐 Cais da Ribeira

Estação de São Bento (São Bento Station)

The station was built in the early 20th century on the site of the convent of São Bento de Avé-Maria, and is worth popping into for a look at the 20,000 tiles (*azulejos*) designed in 1930 by the painter Jorge Colaço in the entrance hall. They depict scenes from the history of railways and transport, and events in Portuguese history. The station is also a good place to get a taxi.

🅐 Praça de Almeida Garrett

Igreja da Misericórdia (Church of the Misericord)

Building of this church started in 1555, with the interior tiles designed in 1629–30; the rococo façade dates from 1750. The small museum attached to the church, Santa Casa da Misericórdia, contains one of the finest paintings in the city, *Fons Vitae* (*Fountain of Life*) of the Flemish school, believed to have been painted in 1520. Rua das Flores was once a place of gold- and silversmiths, and is now full of interesting small shops. The houses date from the 18th century.

Rua das Flores 5 222 074 710 www.scmp.pt Church: 08.00–12.00, 14.30–17.30 Tues–Sun, closed Mon & Aug; Museum: 09.30–12.00, 14.00–17.30 Mon–Fri, closed Sat, Sun & public holidays Metro: line D, S Bento. Admission charge for museum

Igreja de Santa Clara (Church of St Clare)

A charming church, to the east of the cathedral, originally an early 15th-century Franciscan convent. The building has Gothic and baroque elements and a Renaissance portal. Have a look at the 18th-century carved, gilded woodwork inside.

Largo 1° de Decembro 222 054 837 09.30–11.30, 15.00–19.00 Mon–Fri, closed Sat, Sun & public holidays Metro: line D, S Bento

Igreja de São Francisco (Church of St Francis)

If you only have time to visit one church in Porto, make it this one by the side of the Bolsa. It's deconsecrated now and was declared a National Monument in 1984. One of the few existing medieval buildings in Porto, it was built for the Franciscans in the 14th century in the Gothic style with a rose window, but the main attraction is the highly ornate and gilded baroque interior. There is also a small museum in the catacombs, with furniture and a collection of sacred objects. The human bones in the ossuary date from the days before public cemeteries were introduced in Portugal in the 19th century.

Rua Infante D Henrique 222 062 100 09.00–20.00 daily July–Aug, 09.00–19.00 daily June, Sept–Oct, 09.00–18.00 daily Feb–May, 09.00–17.30 daily Nov–Jan Metro: line D, S Bento; Tram: line 1 to Infante. Admission charge

Igreja e Torre dos Clérigos (Clérigos Church and Tower)

Just inside the northern part of the UNESCO area, the baroque church and its tower were built between 1732 and 1773. From the top of the tower (75 m/248 ft high) you get great views of the city. The steps are broad and easy to negotiate, with several views on the way up – be careful though, they're through large openings. Note the unusual elliptical nave in the church.

ⓐ Rua S Filipe de Nery ⓣ 222 001 729 ⓛ Church: 09.00–12.00, 15.30–19.30 Mon–Sat, 10.00–13.00, 21.00–22.00 Sun Apr–Oct; 10.00–13.00, 20.30–22.30 Sun from Nov–Mar; Tower: 09.30–13.00, 14.00–19.00 daily Apr–Oct, 10.00–12.00, 14.00–17.00 daily Nov–Mar ⓜ Metro: line D, S Bento. Admission charge for tower

Mosteiro de Serra do Pilar (Monastery of Serra do Pilar)

Vila Nova de Gaia's main landmark was founded in the 16th century, and this monastery, with a circular church and cloister (most unusual in Portugal), was once the HQ of the future Duke of Wellington. At the beginning of the 20th century, the military connection continued when it became an army barracks. It is still under army control, and the church is difficult to visit (except by arrangement with the tourist office) other than for mass on Sunday mornings. The terrace, however, is open to the public, and affords perhaps the best views of Porto.

ⓐ Largo de Avis ⓣ 223 795 385 ⓜ Metro: line D, Jardim do Morro

Palácio da Bolsa (Stock Exchange Palace)

Just up the hill from the Ribeira waterfront, dominating the western side of the Rua do Infante Dom Henrique is the splendid neoclassical former stock exchange building:

construction began in 1842 on the site of the old São Francisco monastery. The lavishly embellished interior has rooms and public areas decorated in a variety of styles – including a glass-roofed courtyard, the Pátio das Nações, with Roman-inspired mosaic floor and carved granite and marble staircase. The highlight is the extravagant Salão Árabe (Arabian Hall). Although you can enter the building without paying, you can only visit the rooms with a guided tour. In the square itself you will see a monument to Henry the Navigator; to the north, an old market, Mercado Ferreira Borges, is now a venue for events. There is a tourist office to the south of the square, and the late-17th-century church of São Nicolau, with its blue-tiled front.
🅐 Rua Ferreira Borges 🕿 223 399 000 🅦 www.palaciodabolsa.pt 🕒 09.00–19.00 daily Apr–Oct, 09.00–13.00, 14.00–18.00 daily Nov–Mar Ⓝ Metro: line D, S Bento; Tram: line 1 E to Infante

🔵 *The Dom Luís I bridge spans the Douro*

The port lodges of Vila Nova de Gaia

There are over a dozen lodges – where port is aged and matured – owned by shippers, on or near the quayside of Vila Nova de Gaia. Almost all of them offer guided tours and tastings: any admission charge is deducted from the price of what you buy. And they're obviously a good place to buy port. The majority of the firms (many of them originally British) were once family owned, but are now run by international drinks companies. Their names are prominently displayed outside the lodges, and illuminated at night. From Ribeira or central Porto, you'll have to walk across the Luis I bridge, take a taxi or take the metro to Jardim do Morro and then walk down. A more colourful alternative is to be ferried across the Douro. Try to get to them at least 30 minutes before closing times. There are several other good ones to visit, but among the best are:

Graham's Established in the early 19th century, and run by the Symington family for several generations. The family is unusual in owning its own vineyards. They also own other brands such as Dow's and Warre's. The lodge, still working, is behind the quayside, up a hill. The tours are very informative, with tastings of high-quality port; and you can also watch a film about port-making. The terrace offers very good views of Porto.
ⓐ Quinta do Agro 514, Rua Rei Ramiro ⓣ 223 776 330
ⓦ www.symington.com ⓛ 09.30–18.30 daily May–Sept, 09.30–13.00, 14.00–17.30 Mon–Fri, closed Sat & Sun Oct–Apr, closed public holidays

Sandeman On the quayside, and the most conveniently located. The firm (now Portuguese-owned) was founded by Scotsman

George Sandeman in 1790, and is famous for its 'Don' symbol, of a man in a black cloak, one of the first trademark images ever created (in 1928). There's a port museum, a bottle collection and a gift shop. The tour takes around 30 minutes and includes a good film about the making of port.

ⓐ Largo Miguel Bombarda 3 ⓣ 223 740 533/4
ⓦ www.sandeman.com ⓛ 10.00–12.30, 14.00–18.00 daily Mar–Oct, 09.30–12.30, 14.00–17.30 daily Nov–Feb. Admission charge for tour only

Taylor's Founded over 300 years ago, and producing some of the best port around, the firm is still independently owned. After the tour (which is free), with a tasting in the elegant library, you can visit the shop or have lunch in the restaurant – outside in the garden, with its view of Porto, in summer.

ⓐ Rua do Choupelo 250 ⓣ 223 742 800 ⓦ www.taylor.pt
ⓛ 10.00–18.00 Mon–Fri, closed Sat & Sun Sept–June; 10.00–18.00 Mon–Sat, closed Sun July & Aug

CULTURE

Casa do Infante (The House of the Prince)

Once a medieval customs house, dating from 1325, this is the supposed birthplace of Prince Henry the Navigator in 1394. The unpromising 17th-century exterior belies a modern museum in the older part of the building featuring the site's and city's history from Roman times (note the impressive mosaic floor near the ticket desk), using an interactive model of medieval Porto, multimedia, displays of artefacts including ceramics and glass, as well as allusions to the life of Henry the Navigator. Temporary exhibitions are also held there. Last admission 30 minutes before closing times.

ⓐ Rua da Alfândiga 10 ❶ 222 060 400 🕐 10.00–12.30, 14.00–17.30 Tues–Sat, 14.00–17.30 Sun, closed Mon & public holidays ⓜ Metro: line D, S Bento. Admission charge

● *The Sé Catedral (Cathedral) traces its beginnings to the 12th century*

Casa Museu Guerra Junqueiro (Guerra Junqueiro House and Museum)

This baroque house, built in the 18th century, was once the home of the poet Guerra Junqueiro (1850–1923) and contains his collection of art, textiles and artefacts including Islamic works and ceramics. A charming place to visit.

ⓐ Rua D Hugo 32 ⓣ 222 003 689 ⓦ www.cm-porto.pt ⓛ 10.00–12.30, 14.00–17.30 Tues–Sat, 14.00–17.30 Sun, closed Mon & public holidays ⓜ Metro: line D, S Bento. Admission charge

Centro Português de Fotografia (Portuguese Centre for Photography)

This stately yellow building, dating from 1765, was once a prison, but is now the national photographic centre, displaying an archive of old photos of Porto and Lisbon, and exhibits to do with the history of photography. Look out for the high-quality temporary exhibitions.

ⓐ Campo Mártires da Pátria ⓣ 222 076 310 ⓛ 15.00–18.00 Tues–Fri, 15.00–19.00 Sat, Sun & public holidays ⓜ Metro: line D, S Bento. Admission free except for special events

Sé Catedral (Cathedral)

The imposing cathedral, on its dominating hill, was the heart of Porto in the Middle Ages, and is the city's most important historical building. Construction started in the 12th century, in the Romanesque style; the Gothic vestry and the cloister date from the 14th century. Changes made in the 18th century include a silver altarpiece, as well as cloister murals by Nicolau Nasoni. Note also the baroque *azulejos* in the cloister, the crypt and the staircase leading to the fine chapter house. On the terrace, to the south of the cathedral, is the grand bishop's palace, originally built in the 13th century, but heavily remodelled in the late 18th century. To the north is the Torre Medieval. Medieval tower remains were discovered in the 1940s, but this is a reconstruction, moved about 15 m (48 ft) from the original site in the 1950s, and is now the place to book tours through Porto Tours (see page 34).

Terreiro da Sé 222 050 028 Cathedral: 08.45–12.30, 14.30–19.00 Mon–Sat (open 08.30 Sun) Apr–Oct, closes 18.00 Nov–Mar; Cloisters: 09.00–12.15, 14.30–18.00 Mon–Sat Apr–Oct, closes 17.15 Nov–Mar, closed Sun morning Metro: line D, S Bento. Admission charge for cloisters

RETAIL THERAPY

Artesanato dos Clérigos Traditional Portuguese craft objects and regional costumes. Rua da Assunção 33–34 222 000 257 09.30–12.30, 14.30–19.00 Mon–Fri (09.30–13.00 Sat Nov–May, (09.30–19.00 Sat June–Oct), closed Sun

Casa das Cestinhas One of the best places to go for local handicrafts. Cais de Ribeira 34 222 001 690 09.00–19.00 Mon–Sat, closed Sun

CRAT (Centro Regional de Artes Tradicionals) In a 17th-century building, this is the official centre for traditional local workmanship. Rua de Reboleira 37 223 390 144 10.00–12.00, 13.00–18.00 Mon–Fri, closed Sat, Sun & public holidays

Galeria de Artesanato O Galo High-quality ceramics by local designers. ⓐ Rua Mouzinho de Silveira 68 ⓣ 223 325 294 ⓛ 09.30–12.30, 13.30–19.00 Mon–Fri, 09.30–13.00 Sat

Garrafeira Clériporto A good place to buy port, near the Clérigos Tower. ⓐ Rua da Assunção 38 ⓣ 222 038 026

Loja do Infante A large selection of port is on sale in this building dating back to the 14th and 15th centuries. ⓐ Rua Infante D Henrique 53 ⓣ 222 051 341 ⓛ 10.30–13.30, 14.30–19.00 Mon–Sat, closed Sun

TAKING A BREAK

A Canastra da Ribeira £ ❶ A small restaurant with stone walls and beamed ceilings, where you can also sit outdoors and get a drink outside dining hours. Try the fried octopus or the sardines. ⓐ Cais de Ribeira 37 ⓣ 222 080 180 ⓛ 12.00–15.30, 18.30–22.30 daily ⓜ Metro: line D, S Bento

Café do Cais £ ❷ This recent, and very popular, addition to Porto's café scene is just along from the Ribeira quay. It's basically a glass box (though it also has a terrace) from which you can sip your coffee and look at the port lodges of Gaia. ⓐ Cais da Estiva ⓣ 222 088 385 ⓛ varies seasonally

Bogani Café £–££ ❸ One of the trendiest new places in Gaia, with Philippe Starck furnishings. Right on the quay. ⓐ Cais de Gaia ⓣ 223 747 0700 ⓛ varies seasonally

O Comercial ££ ❹ In the Palácio da Bolsa, with its fine interior. Very good Portuguese food in a formal setting – and a view of the church of São Francisco. ⓐ Palácio da Bolsa, Rua Ferreira Borges ☏ 223 322 019 🕑 12.30–15.00, 20.00–23.00 Mon–Sat, closed Sun Ⓜ Metro: line D, S Bento

AFTER DARK

Restaurants
Adega e Presuntaria Transmontana II ££ ❺ Grilled and smoked meat is the speciality in this popular, stone-walled Gaia restaurant. ⓐ Rua Candido dos Reis 132 ☏ 223 597 792 🕑 12.30–15.00, 19.30–23.00 daily

Chez Lapin ££ ❻ There's been a restaurant in this former stables on the Ribeira quay since 1910. You can eat outside, downstairs (decorated with football memorabilia) or upstairs (with its old lampshades, and graffiti and business cards, memos, etc. on the walls). Service is friendly, and the food (try the roasted octopus) excellent. ⓐ Rua dos Canastreiros 42 ☏ 222 006 418 🕑 12.30–15.00, 19.00–23.30 daily Ⓜ Metro: line D, S Bento

Dom Tonho ££ ❼ Rather more expensive than many of Ribeira's restaurants, but it's a fashionable spot belonging to the Portuguese pop star Rui Veloso, and the modern interior, with its exposed granite walls, totally belies the exterior. High-quality, creative and well-presented food featuring ingredients such as rabbit (with coriander) and kid in various guises. There's a bar downstairs. ⓐ Cais de Ribeira 13–15 ⓣ 222 004 307 ⓛ 12.30–14.45, 19.30–23.15 daily ⓜ Metro: line D, S Bento

Horta dos Reis ££ ⓑ A favourite for local parties with its gardens and view from Gaia over to Ribeira, and best visited in summer. A lively atmosphere and particularly good fish and seafood. ⓐ Rua Camilo Castelo Branco 947 ⓣ 223 770 324 ⓛ 12.30–15.00, 19.30–23.00 Mon–Sat, closed Sat lunch & Sun

Bars & clubs
Aniki-Bóbó One of the most fashionable clubs in town, often with live music. ⓐ Rua da Fonte Taurina 36–38 ⓣ 223 324 619 ⓛ 21.00–02.00 Tues–Sat, closed Sun–Mon

Hard Club In Gaia, and one of the city's main live music venues. ⓐ Cais de Gaia 1158 ⓣ 223 744 755 ⓛ 22.00–04.00 Wed–Sat, closed Sun–Tues

Ribeirinha One of the oldest bars in Ribeira, crowded and cheerful. ⓐ Rua de São João 70–72 ⓣ 223 322 572 ⓛ 22.00–02.00 daily

Ryan's Irish Pub Just what the name says and often packed. ⓐ Rua Infante D Henrique 18 ⓣ 222 005 366 ⓛ Late nights: 10.00–02.00 Thur & Sun, 21.00–04.00 Fri, 17.00–04.00 Sat ⓘ There's a cover charge after 23.00.

The city centre

The city centre is the heart of Porto's commercial life, and the main shopping district. The attractive squares and streets (several of them pedestrianised), with their mixture of different architectural styles, are well worth wandering around to get a feel for the life of modern Porto. It's also where you will find banks, some of the main performance venues and two of the city's three tourist offices. And you can't fail to notice the area's patterned pavements, made of limestone and basalt – and slippery in the rain.

SIGHTS & ATTRACTIONS

There are few formal attractions in the city centre, but many interesting 19th- and 20th-century buildings, though some of those dating from the 1950s to the 1970s are pretty functional, and now somewhat faded.

The focal point here is the mainly neoclassical and art nouveau **Avenida dos Aliados**, with one square, the Praça do General Humberto, at the north end and another, the Praça da Liberdade, at the south. The north end is dominated by the **Câmara Municipal** (Town Hall; also known as Paços do Concelho), which may look as if it's been there for centuries, but was completed only in 1957. The equestrian statue in **Praça da Liberdade** is of the 19th-century King Pedro IV, unveiled in 1866.

To the east of the square is the colourful two-tiered, mainly wrought-iron, 19th-century **Mercado do Bolhão** (Bolhão food market). A little further to the east is the **Rua de Santa Catarina**, the main shopping street. Look out for the Majestic café at No 112, with its fine 1920s interior, and the striking exterior tiles of the simple, early-18th-century **Capela das Almas** at No 428. The tiles on this chapel date only from 1929 (restored in 1982), and depict the lives of Saints Francis and Catherine. The street also has a major shopping centre. In the Rua de Passos Manuel is the **Coliseu**, a former cinema, and now a major venue for high-profile performances. A little further to the south is the pleasant Praça de Batalha, with its fountain, where you will find the **Teatro Nacional de São João**, built in 1909.

To the west of the Praça da Liberdade, near the Hospital Santo Antonio, is a small park, the **Jardim Cordoaria**. The area also has several buildings which are part of the university.

🔺 *The Praça da Liberdade is a focal point for the city centre*

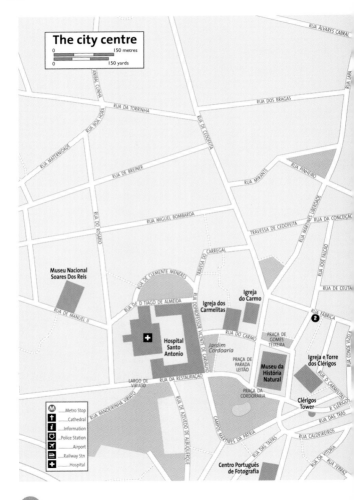

The city centre

| 0 | 150 metres |
| 0 | 150 yards |

RUA ÁLVARES CABRAL

RUA DA TORRINHA

RUA DOS BRAGAS

ANÍBAL CUNHA

RUA BOA HORA

RUA LAVA

RUA DE CEDOFEITA

RUA MATERNIDADE

RUA DE BREINER

RUA MIRANTE

RUA PINHEIRO

RUA MIGUEL BOMBARDA

RUA MARTINS LIBERDADE

RUA DA CONCEIÇÃO

RUA DO ROSÁRIO

TRAVESSA DE CEDOFEITA

CARREGAL

RUA JOSÉ FALCÃO

Museu Nacional Soares Dos Reis

RUA DE CLEMENTE MENERES

RUA DE CEUTA

Igreja do Carmo

RUA DE D TIAGO DE ALMEIDA

RUA DE MANUEL II

RUA DOM PROFESSOR VICENTE DE CARVALHO

Igreja dos Carmelitas

RUA FÁBRICA

2

RUA DO CARMO

PRAÇA DE GOMES TEIXEIRA

✚ **Hospital Santo Antonio**

Jardim Cordoaria

Igreja e Torre dos Clérigos

PRAÇA DE PARADA LEITÃO

Museu da História Natural

RUA D'CARMELITAS

LARGO DE VIRIATO

RUA DA RESTAURAÇÃO

PRAÇA DA CORDORARIA

Clérigos Tower

R CLÉRIGOS

RUA BANDEIRINHA VIRIATO

RUA DE AZEVEDO DE ALBUQUERQUE

RUA DAS TRÁS

Ⓜ	Metro Stop
✝	Cathedral
𝒊	Information
🛡	Police Station
✈	Airport
▤	Railway Stn
✚	Hospital

CAMPOS MÁRTYRES DA PÁTRIA

RUA DAS TAIPAS

RUA CALDEIREIROS

RUA DA VITÓRIA

RUA FERRAZ

Centro Português de Fotografia

Hospital Santo Antonio

The exterior of this imposing building, with its six Doric columns, is well worth a look at. One of the city's main hospitals, built 1790–1825, it was designed by English architect John Carr, who was the first to introduce the British neo-Palladian style to Porto.
🅐 Largo Prof Abel Salazar Ⓝ Metro: line D, S Bento

Igreja do Carmo (Carmo Church)

This former monastery is one of the outstanding rococo buildings in Porto. Of especial interest are the unusual balcony on the main façade, and the richly decorated *azulejos*, on the side of the building, which refer to the life of the Virgin Mary. The pediment at the top of the main façade features figures representing the four Evangelists. Step inside to admire the ornate interior.
🅐 Rua do Carmo ⓣ 222 078 400 Ⓛ 08.00–12.00, 14.00–17.00 Mon–Fri, 08.00–12.00 Sat, 07.30–13.00 Sun Ⓝ Metro: line D, S Bento

Igreja dos Carmelitas (Church of the Carmelites)

This former convent, built in the early 17th century with considerable alterations made a century later, includes a main chapel built by master mason António da Silva. The interior is mainly in the rococo style. The rather solemn façade is mid-18th century.
🅐 Rua do Carmo ⓣ 222 050 279 Ⓛ 08.30–11.00, 15.00–17.00 Mon–Sat, 17.00–19.00 Sun Ⓝ Metro: line D, S Bento

Igreja de Santa Ildefonso (Church of St Ildefonso)

In the Praça da Batalha, it's worth quickly popping into this

⬤ *The 18th-century Capela das Almas features superb examples of* azulejos peaceful and essentially simple church built from 1709–39, with its polygonal nave (with a wooden ceiling), baroque elements in the interior and exterior tiles dating from 1932.

ⓐ Praça da Batalha ⓣ 222 004 366 ⓛ 09.00–12.00, 15.00–18.30 Mon–Fri, 09.00–12.00, 15.00–20.00 Sat, 09.00–12.45, 18.00–19.45 Sun ⓝ Metro: line D, S Bento

CULTURE

Museu da História Natural (Natural History Museum)

This fine neoclassical building was completed in the late 19th century, and is now part of the university's Faculty of Sciences. There are two exhibition halls open to the public: Archaeology and Palaeontology, and Mineralogy.

ⓐ Praça Gomes Teixeira ⓣ 223 401 400 ⓛ Archaeology and Palaeontology: 10.00–12.00 Mon–Fri; Mineralogy 14.30–16.30 Mon–Fri, closed public holidays ⓝ Metro: line D, S Bento

Museu Nacional Soares Dos Reis (Soares Dos Reis Museum)

Porto's main museum: home to collections of both visual and decorative arts, and pleasantly bright and unstuffy after recent renovation. Formerly the Palácio dos Carrancas, once a wealthy merchant's residence, and built at the end of the 18th century, it became a royal palace in the mid-19th century and later Portugal's first fine arts museum. Paintings and sculptures on the first floor (including the work of 19th-century sculptor António Soares Dos Reis, after whom the museum is named) are by Portuguese artists from the 19th century to the mid-20th century, as well as foreigners who produced works in Portugal.

Look out for old views of Porto and the Douro, and the works of Henrique Pousão; sculptures date from as far back as the medieval period. The decorative arts section on the second floor

⬥ *The Doric colonnade of Hospital Santo Antonio*

includes ceramics, glass, jewellery, textiles and furniture, both
Portuguese and foreign, dating from the 17th to the 20th century.
The museum also holds major temporary exhibitions. The
attractive tiled courtyard is used as a café in summer.
Rua D Manuel II 44 223 393 770 www.ipmuseus.pt
14.00–18.00 Tues, 10.00–18.00 Wed–Sun, closed Mon
Bus: 3, 6, 20, 24, 35, 37, 52, 78, 500 to Miragaia. Admission
charge (free until 14.00 Sun & public holidays)

RETAIL THERAPY

A Pérola do Bolhão With a striking art nouveau façade, this food
store – selling cheese, sausages, salt cod, port and other
specialities – was founded in 1917 opposite the entrance to
Bolhão market. Rua Formosa 279 222 004 009 09.30–
13.00, 15.00–19.30 Mon–Fri, 09.30–13.00 Sat, closed Sun

Arcadia Established in 1933, one of the best places to buy
pastries, chocolate and confectionery. Rua Almada 63 222
001 518 09.30–19.00 Mon–Fri, 09.30–13.00 Sat, closed Sun

Armazém dos Linhos Founded in the late 19th century, selling
linen and decorative woven fabrics. Rua de Passos Manuel 19
222 004 750 09.30–12.30, 14.30–19.00 Mon–Thur,
10.00–12.30, 14.30–19.00 Fri, 10.00–13.00 Sat, closed Sun

Canjirão Portuguese handicrafts. Rua de Santo Ildefonso 215
222 008 523 10.00–12.15, 15.15–19.15 Mon–Fri, 10.00–13.00
Sat, closed Sun

Cerâmica Kico Craft objects, including ceramics. ⓐ Rua de Santa Catarina 212 ⓣ 222 059 162 ⓛ 10.00–19.30 Mon–Sat, closed Sun

Garrafeira do Carmo One of the city's best port and wine shops, with vintage port going back to 1900. ⓐ Rua do Carmo 17–18 ⓣ 222 003 285 ⓛ 09.00–13.00, 14.00–19.00 Mon–Sat, closed Sun

Livraria Lello As much a sight as a bookshop. Over a century old, and with a stunning art nouveau interior, dominated by a grand wooden staircase, it specialises in art books (many in English), as well as books about Porto, and maps. There are a few tables upstairs where you can get a drink or a pastry. ⓐ Rua das Carmelitas 144 ⓣ 222 018 170 ⓛ 10.00–19.30 Mon–Sat, closed Sun

Memórias A good craft shop, near S Bento station. ⓐ Rua das Flores 18 ⓣ 222 0856 726 ⓛ 09.30–12.30, 14.30–19.00 Mon–Fri, 10.00–13.00 Sat, closed Sun

Via Catarina One of Porto's main shopping centres, selling mainly clothes. Bars and cafés on the top floor (level 4). ⓐ Rua de Santa Catarina 312–350 ⓣ 222 075 600 ⓛ shops: 10.00–22.00 daily; food outlets: 09.00–23.00 daily

TAKING A BREAK

Café Guarany £ ❶ Founded in 1933, a musicians' haunt with live music in the evenings, and good value food and drinks. ⓐ Avenida dos Aliados 85–89 ⓣ 223 321 272 ⓛ 09.00–24.00 daily ⓝ Metro: line D, Aliados

Café Progresso £ ❷ Opened in 1899, and a local institution. ⓐ Rua Actor João Guedes 5 ❶ 223 322 647 ⏱ 07.00–19.00 Mon–Thur, 07.00–24.00 Fri & Sat, closed Sun ⓜ Metro: line D, S Bento

Café Majestic £–££ ❸ Come to this famous café, with its 1920s interior and uniformed waiters, for a coffee and a pastry ... or something a bit more substantial. ⓐ Rua de Santa Catarina 112 ❶ 222 003 887 ⏱ 09.30–24.00 Mon–Sat, closed Sun ⓜ Metro: lines A, B, C, E Bolhão

Ribeiro £–££ ❹ One of the best places for traditional food in the city centre, in a semi-rustic setting. Try the *bacalhau*, or maybe the tripe if you're up to it. ⓐ Praça Porveiros 2 ❶ 222 008 637 ⏱ 12.00–15.00, 19.00–23.00 daily ⓜ Metro: line D, S Bento or Bolhão

AFTER DARK

Restaurants
Abadia do Porto £ ❺ Large, simple and lively, serving straight-forward local cuisine. ⓐ Rua Ateneu Comercial 22 ❶ 222 008 757 ⏱ 12.00–23.00 Mon–Sat, closed Sun ⓜ Metro: line D, S Bento

Café Concerto Rivoli £ ❻ A good, popular, budget choice for Portuguese specialities. ⓐ Praça Dom João I ❶ 223 392 200 ⏱ 12.30–15.00, 19.30–23.00 daily ⓜ Metro: line D, Aliados

O Escondidinho ££ ❼ Well-prepared local food, particularly the fish and seafood. Also decent meat dishes, some from further afield. @ Rua Passos Manuel 144 ☎ 222 001 079 🕙 12.00–15.00, 19.00–22.00 Mon–Sat, closed Sun Ⓜ Metro: line D, S Bento

Tripeiro ££ ❽ Hearty local cuisine, including tripe, as the name suggests. @ Rua de Passos Manuel 195 ☎ 222 005 886 🕙 12.00–15.00, 19.00–22.00 Mon–Sat, closed Sun Ⓜ Metro: line D, S Bento

Portucale £££ ❾ Generally considered one of the best restaurants in Porto (serving Portuguese cuisine and luxury ingredients) with a 13th-floor location, offering superb views, as well as fine food. @ Rua da Alegria 596 ☎ 225 370 717 🕙 12.30–14.30, 19.30–22.00 daily Ⓜ Metro: lines A, B, C, E Bolhão

Bars & clubs
There are many bars in the area, though a lot of them close early. Below are two noteworthy ones:

Cinema Batalha With two trendy bars and a terrace. @ Praça de Batalha 47 ☎ 222 011 913 🕙 12.00–02.00 during week, to 04.00 at weekends

Maus Hábitos A cultural centre with a restaurant and a lively bar. @ Rua Passos Manuel 178 (4th floor) ☎ 222 087 268 🕙 until 02.00 Tues–Sun

West of the city centre

Many of Porto's most appealing museums and attractions are
to the west of the city centre and the World Heritage area –
either along the Douro or in the Boavista area. Both areas offer a
striking contrast to crowded Ribeira and the bustling city centre.
In Boavista, the roads and avenues are broad and leafy, with
some of the best modern hotels, and classy shops, as well as the
homes of Porto's wealthier inhabitants. In Foz do Douro,
normally referred to simply as Foz, the riverside and the
seashore are more like a resort area, with waterfront restaurants
and cafés. The large villas lining the streets leading downhill are
among the most exclusive in the city. Western Porto is currently
not well served by the metro, except to the north, so you'll need
to gear up for some serious walking or rely on buses or taxis.

SIGHTS & ATTRACTIONS

The Boavista area starts at the Rotunda da Boavista (officially
called Praça Mouzinho de Albuquerque, a name rarely used), a
busy roundabout, with a small park in the centre, 3 km (2 miles)
northwest of Praça da Liberdade. The middle of the park is
dominated by a tall column commemorating the Peninsular
War (1808–14) and the victory over the French. It was actually
built in 1951. Just to the north of the roundabout is the new
Casa da Música. And nearby are two shopping centres. The
Avenida da Boavista runs 8 km (5 miles) from the Rotunda to the
Atlantic and Foz do Douro, passing the Parque da Cidade –
Porto's biggest green space. The equestrian statue near the sea

is of the early-19th-century king João VI looking towards Brazil. Along the avenue, note the grand late-19th-century houses built by returning Portuguese who had made their fortunes in Brazil. They often have palm trees in their gardens, to remind their owners of the New World. The area also has several fine 1930s houses, and cutting-edge modern buildings.

Around 2 km (1 mile) to the south of the Rotunda, and not far from the UNESCO area are a cluster of museums near the Douro, as well as the Palácio de Cristal park.

The Foz do Douro area is to the west of the concrete Ponte de Arrábida, with its 270-m (885-ft) span. There are few formal sights or attractions, but the area is particularly pleasant with walks (you'll also see many joggers) by the mouth of the river and the Atlantic, small beaches (where you are advised not to swim) and lively nightlife in summer, particularly on the Avenida do Brasil, and its continuation (towards Ribeira) the Avenida de Dom Carlos I. The two forts on the coast are the Castelo do Queijo, at the end of the Avenida da Boavista, and Castelo de São João, further east.

Casa da Música (House of Music)

After years of delay, the hugely impressive and spankingly modern polyhedron-shaped Casa da Música, designed by Dutch architect Rem Koolhaas, finally opened in 2005. Porto's new concert hall and opera house is now the base of the Orquestra Nacional do Porto, and has fast become a major centre of local cultural life.
ⓐ Rotonda da Boavista ⓣ 220 120 220
ⓦ www.casadamusica.com ⓝ Metro: lines A, B, C, E Casa da Música

Francisco Sá Carneiro

RAMALDE

VISO

Parque de Campismo da Prelada

VIA DE CINTURA INTERNA IC23

Boavista Football Club

AVENIDA DA BOAVISTA

BOAVISTA

Casa da Música

Monumento a Guerra Peninsular

ROTUNDA DA BOAVISTA

Cemitério de Agramonte

Igreja de São Martinho de Cedofeita

Jardim Botânico

LORDELO DO OURO

RUA DOS SOBREIRAS

Museu do Carro Eléctrico

Casa Tait

Museu Romântico

Ponte da Arrábida

Palácio de Cristal

Museu do Vinho Porto

Rio Douro

Alfandega Nova

Museu dos Transportes e Comunicações

91

Castelo do Queijo ('Cheese Castle')

The name of this 17th-century fort literally means 'cheese castle', because the rocks on which it is built are thought to resemble cheese. Officially it's the fortress of S Francisco Xavier. You might want to pop in for the view and the small café.

ⓐ Praça de Gonçalves Zarco ❶ 226 181 067 ⏰ 13.00–18.00 Tues–Sun, closed Mon ⓦ Bus: 200. Admission charge

Igreja de São Martinho de Cedofeita
(Church of St Martino de Cedofeita)

Near the Rotunda da Boavista, and once the centre of a hamlet which was eventually absorbed into the city, this early-13th-

● *The Casa da Música (House of Music) hosts international performances*

century Romanesque church was built on the remains of an earlier temple. The simple church is one of the few of its type in Portugal.

ⓐ Largo do Priorado ① 222 005 620 ⓛ 09.00–12.00, 16.00–19.30 Mon–Sat, 09.00–12.00 Sun Ⓝ Metro: lines A, B, C, E Carolina Michaelis

Palácio de Cristal (Crystal Palace)

The shady park – with many pleasant walks, a pond, educational children's activities, a play area and views of Porto – was laid out in the late 19th century by architect Emile David. It was the site of a crystal palace (hence its name) designed by the British architect Thomas Dillen Jones for the international exhibition of 1865. This was pulled down, against local protests, and replaced by the present Rosa Mota pavilion, which is used for sporting, musical and other events, in 1956. The pavilion also has a restaurant. The new Biblioteca Municipal Almeida Garrett (public library), with free internet access, and an art gallery are also in the grounds of the park.

ⓐ Rua Dom Manuel II (main entrance) ① 225 430 360
ⓛ 09.00–18.00 daily Apr–Sept, 09.00–17.00 daily Oct–Mar
Ⓝ Bus: 3, 20, 37, 52, 78

Parque da Cidade (City Park)

The 50-hectare (124-acre) park leads straight down to the sea. It has lakes, a waterfall, lawns, woodland, a belvedere for the view, mini-golf and several activities (such as ponies for hire) that might attract children.

ⓐ Avenida da Boavista ⓛ daylight hours Ⓝ Bus: 19, 24, 36, 200

CULTURE

Casa Tait (Tait House)

This fine house, once British-owned, and right next to the Museu Romântico, has lovely gardens, and a collection of old coins. It is also used for special events and exhibitions. Last admission 30 minutes before closing.

ⓐ Rua de Entre Quintas 219 ⓣ 226 057 000 ⓛ 10.00–12.30, 14.00–17.30 Tues–Fri, 14.00–18.00 Sat & Sun ⓝ Bus: 3, 20, 37, 52, 78; Tram: 1E Massarelos

Fundacão de Serralves Museu de Arte Contemporânea de Serralves (Serralves Foundation Museum of Contemporary Art)

Just off the Avenida da Boavista, and the highlight, for many, of a trip to Porto: somewhere you could easily spend most of a day. The 18-hectare (45-acre) park, created by the wealthy Carlos Alberto Carbral, who lived there, was acquired by the Portuguese state in 1986; a foundation involving local companies and other organisations was set up three years later to run it. The exciting, all-white art museum, with its many angular spaces, and an auditorium, was designed by Alvaro Siza Viera, and opened in 1999. Alongside the permanent collection, with works by some big names, major themed temporary international exhibitions change every three months or so.

But there's much more to the Serralves than the works of art on display: two excellent shops with art books, design objects and gifts, a café with a terrace, which becomes a more formal restaurant in the evening, a bar, and many special events and performances through the year.

The park itself, with quirky sculptures dotted around, features a formal French garden, a wilder English one and a 'farm', with animals, that children will enjoy. There is also a café in the grounds, and jazz concerts in July. Unfortunately, you can't picnic in the park.

The art deco **Casa de Serralves**, the luxurious pink villa of the former owners, was built between 1920 and 1940, and the superb interior, with its central gallery, impressive marble bathroom and parquet floors is one of the finest of its type. The building now houses temporary exhibitions and other events. ⓐ Rua D João de Castro 210 ⓣ 226 156 500

🔺 *Dig this – surreal art at the Fundacão Park*

www.serralves.pt 10.00–19.00 Tues–Thur, 10.00–22.00 Fri & Sat, 10.00–20.00 Sun & holidays, closed Mon Apr–Sept; 10.00–19.00 Tues–Sun, closed Mon Oct–Mar Bus: 19, 21, 30, 78, 201, 207. Admission charge (free 10.00–14.00 Sun) for park and museum or park only

Museu do Carro Eléctrico (Tram Museum)

Porto was the first city in the Iberian peninsula to have a tram system, and this museum – in an old electrical power station next to the STCP tram depot by the Douro – opened in 1992. It's a fun place to go, and features trams and other vehicles dating back to the 19th century. It also has a shop and a café, and stages special events.

Almeda Basílio Teles 51 226 158 185 www.museu-carro-electrico-stcp.pt 09.30–12.30, 14.30–18.00 Tues–Fri; 15.00–19.00 Sat, Sun & public holidays, open Mon by arrangement only Tram: 1E, 18 Massarelos; Bus: 1, 3, 6, 7, 14, 15, 19, 20, 36, 37, 38, 39, 41, 58, 60, 77. Admission charge

Museu dos Transportes e Communicações (Transport and Communications Museum)

A little way west of Ribeira, in a huge customs house built in 1860, the collection is mainly devoted to cars – and how they work, their history, future and impact on society. Many of the intriguing exhibits are interactive. Also a good café/bar.

Rua Nova da Alfândega 223 403 000 www.amtc.pt 10.00–12.00, 14.00–18.00 Tues–Fri, 15.00–19.00 Sat, Sun & public holidays, closed Mon Tram: 1E Alfândega. Admission charge

⬥ *Escape from the city for the coast, at Foz do Douro*

Museu do Vinho Porto (Port Museum)

Opened in 2004, this contemporary museum (with some interactive activities for children) celebrating the history of port, is westward along the quayside from Ribeira. Housed in an 18th-century wine warehouse, it's well worth visiting for its elegantly presented displays.

ⓐ Rua do Monchique 45–52 ⓣ 222 076 300 ⓛ 11.00–19.00 Tues–Sun, closed Mon & public holidays ⓝ Tram: 1E Alfândega. Admission charge

Museu Romântico (Romantic Museum)

The early-19th-century Quinta de Machierinha with its delightful gardens is one of the most pleasing sights in Porto. The house was once in the countryside, but now displays the kind of interiors typically found in a wealthy 19th-century merchant's town house. It is also dedicated to Carlos Alberto, the exiled king of Piedmont-Sardinia, who died there in 1849. Visits in small groups only, so you might have to wait ten minutes or so. Last admission 30 minutes before closing.

Downstairs is the Solar do Vinho Porto, where you can enjoy a glass of port from a huge selection – either in the elegant lounge or on the pretty terrace, with its views of the Douro. You can get to the house either downhill via the gardens of the Palácio de Cristal or through the main entrance.

ⓐ Rua de Entre Quintas 220 ⓣ 226 057 033 ⓛ Museum: 10.00–12.30, 14.00–17.30 Tues–Sat, 14.00–17.30 Sun, closed Mon & public holidays; Solar do Vinho Porto: 14.00–20.00 Mon–Thur, 14.00–24.00 Fri & Sat, closed Sun ⓝ Bus: 3, 20, 37, 52, 78; Tram: 1E Massarelos. Admission charge for museum (except Sat and Sun)

RETAIL THERAPY

There are two good shopping centres near the Rotunda da Boavista:

Centro Comercial Cidade do Porto (with four cinema screens) has food shops, a supermarket, a tobacconist, a pharmacy, perfumeries, an internet café and clothes shops such as Mango, Zara and Acessorize. ⓐ Praça do Bom Sucesso 61 ⓣ 226 006 584 🕙 10.00–23.00 daily

Galeria Comercial Peninsula has mainly clothes shops including Max Mara, Gant and Massimo Dutti. ⓐ Praça do Bom Sucesso 159 ⓣ 226 001 862 🕙 10.00–23.00 daily

TAKING A BREAK

Portugalia £ ❶ Part of a national chain, but with a great view of the mouth of the Douro. Good steaks and seafood, and popular with children. You can get just a sandwich or a drink. ⓐ Rua do Passeio Alegre ⓣ 225 321 271 🕙 12.00–24.00 daily ⓝ Bus: 200

Cafeína £–££ ❷ An atmospheric café, bar and restaurant in the Foz area with excellent creative food and a pleasant atmosphere. Fashionable and youngish, with jazz playing in the background. ⓐ Rua do Padrão 100 ⓣ 226 108 059 🕙 10.00–02.00 daily ⓝ Bus: 200

Fundação Serralves £–££ ❸ You can visit the museum's café for either a buffet lunch, or a drink (there's also a bar downstairs) or a more formal meal when it turns into a restaurant in the evening. **ⓐ** Rua D João de Castro 210 **ⓣ** Restaurant reservations: 226 170 355 **ⓛ** Café: 12.00–19.00 daily; Restaurant: 20.00–24.00 daily **ⓝ** Bus: 19, 21, 30, 78, 201, 207

Restaurante Bar da Praia do Ourigo £–££ **❹** Right by the Atlantic next to a beach in Foz, glass-fronted, with a terrace. Good seafood, and a great location. **ⓐ** Foz do Douro (by Av do Brasil) **ⓣ** 226 189 593 **ⓛ** Food served 12.00–15.00, 20.00–23.30 daily; bar open until 02.00 **ⓝ** Bus: 200

AFTER DARK

Restaurants
Casa Agricola ££ **❺** With a lively café/bar downstairs, this is an atmospheric restaurant, with friendly service, providing traditional and more international dishes, such as pasta, magret of duck and roast beef. The wine list is also very impressive. If you're feeling hungry try one of their filling *asçordas* (bread stews). **ⓐ** Rua Bom Sucesso 241–243 **ⓣ** 226 053 350 **ⓛ** Restaurant: 12.30–15.00, 20.00–22.30 Mon–Sat, closed Sun **ⓝ** Metro: lines A, B, C, E Casa da Música

Casa do Marechal ££ **❻** Top-notch Portuguese food. **ⓐ** Avenida da Boavista 2674 **ⓣ** 226 104 702 **ⓛ** 12.30–15.00, 19.00–22.00 daily **ⓝ** Bus: 19, 21, 30, 78, 201, 207

Churrascão do Mar ££ **❼** One of the best fish and seafood restaurants in town. In an impressive old house. **ⓐ** Rua João

Grave 134–152 ☏ 226 068 458 ⏱ 12.30–15.00, 19.00–23.00 Mon–Sat, closed Sun 🚍 Bus: 19, 21, 30, 78, 201, 207

Bull & Bear £££ ❽ In a modern building, serving celebrated creative cuisine, giving the local staples a new twist. 🅐 Avenida da Boavista 3431 ☏ 226 107 669 ⏱ 12.30–15.00, 20.00–22.30 daily, closed Sat & Sun lunch 🚍 Bus: 19, 21, 30, 78, 201, 207

Foz Velha £££ ❾ A local favourite for anniversaries and birthdays, with extremely high-quality modern food in a formal atmosphere. 🅐 Esplanada Castelo 141 ☏ 226 154 178 ⏱ 12.30–15.00, 19.30–23.00 Wed–Mon, closed Tues, & Wed lunch 🚍 Bus: 200

Bars & clubs

You'll find some of the most happening places in Porto in this area. Here are a few of them:

Bar Bazaar Not far from the Palácio de Cristal, on the river. 🅐 Cais das Pedras 13 ☏ 226 062 113 ⏱ 16.00–02.00 daily

New Yorker The mellow piano bar of the Sheraton hotel is a lively meeting place, particularly at weekends. And prices are reasonable for a 5-star hotel. 🅐 Rua Tenente Valadim 146 ☏ 220 404 000 ⏱ 10.00–02.00 daily

Pop In Foz, one of the smoothest clubs in Porto. 🅐 Rua Padre Luis Cabral 1090 ☏ 226 183 959 ⏱ 23.00–04.00 Thur–Sat, closed Sun–Wed

Trintaeum In an old building, but an up-to-the-minute interior, one of the best discos in town – in the Foz area. ⓐ Rua do Passeio Alegre 564 ⓣ 226 107 567 ⓒ 22.30–02.00 Mon–Thur, 22.30–04.00 Fri & Sat, closed Sun

Triplex This restaurant (one of the better ones in Porto) and bar covers three floors of a 19th-century building. ⓐ Avenida da Boavista 911 ⓣ 226 063 163/4 ⓒ 12.30–03.00 Mon–Sat, closed Sun

Twins A favourite for pretty party people. ⓐ Rua Passeio Alegre 1000 ⓣ 226 195 352 ⓒ 23.00–04.00 daily

🔽 *Foz harbour*

▶ *Braga Café*

OUT OF TOWN
trips

Guimarães

'Aqui Nasceu Portugal,' says a sign on the side of a building as you walk into the centre of town: 'Portugal was born here'. And, indeed, in many ways it was, as every Portuguese schoolchild knows. The city, mostly industrial now, with textile and shoe factories among others, was the birthplace of Afonso Henriques (in 1110), the first real king of the country. It became the capital of Portucale, and a base for the defeat of the Moors and the eventual establishment of what is now Portugal. The 65,000 people who live here are proud of its past, and looking forward to its future since the old town centre was put on the UNESCO World Heritage List in 2001, and the city was nominated as a European Capital of Culture for 2012. Those accolades, along with the Euro 2004 football championships (Guimarães has an important club and ground), have led to a considerable improvement of the local infrastructure, tourist facilities and travel connections.

The town was founded in the 10th century, when the local monastery attracted a settlement and the castle was built for its defence. Rua de Santa Maria evolved to link the two. Because of the monastery, which grew in importance, the town also became a centre of pilgrimage, and walls were erected to protect it (though they were mostly pulled down in the 19th century). The layout of the town centre today is much as it was in the 15th century; most of the buildings you'll see when you wander around the highly attractive historic centre today date from the 17th century. Guimarães was granted the status of a city in 1853; it is also home to a major university. The main event,

⬥ *The pretty streets of Guimarães*

Porto region

the Festas de Cidade e Gualterianas on the first weekend of August, dates back to 1452. There is also a classical music festival in late May and June, and the important Jazz Festival in November.

GETTING THERE

Guimarães, in the Minho province, is around 60 km (37 miles) northeast from central Porto. The best way to get there from Porto is by train from S Bento or Campanhã stations; fares are modest, and the journey takes a little over an hour in clean, punctual trains. You can also drive via the A3 or go by bus (a number of bus companies operating in Porto go there), but it can take two hours. You can park (outside the UNESCO area), including at the railway station and the Vila Flor nearby. The bus station is to the southwest of the city centre, about 15 minutes' walk. The train station is also to the south, a short walk from the historic centre.

The main tourist office is **Posto de Turismo da Almeda** (ⓐ Almeda de S Dâmaso 83 ⓣ 253 412 450 ⓛ 09.30–12.30, 14.00–18.30 Mon–Fri, closed Sat & Sun); **Posto de Turismo** (ⓐ Praça de Santiago 37 ⓣ 253 518 790 ⓛ 09.30–18.30 Mon–Sat, 10.00–13.00 Sun) is in the old town.

The tourism website is ⓦ www.guimaraesturismo.com

You can hire an MP3 audio-guide in English about the old town from the Posto de Turismo.

SIGHTS & ATTRACTIONS

The primary attraction is the mainly pedestrianised historic centre and its atmospheric cobbled streets and squares, with their pretty houses. The squares – Largo da Oliveira, Praça de Santiago and Largo João Franco – all have several enticing cafés. You'll notice that none of the houses has a TV aerial or satellite dish – the result of local incentives to preserve the look of the place. The city has also bought a number of buildings in the old town and put them to new use to ensure their future. As a result there is a pleasing coherence to Guimarães, with a real sense of the past. You should easily be able to get around it in half a day, but allow a full day if you want to visit all the museums. The gardens by the castle and the ducal palace are a very pleasant place to take a break. As you walk around you'll see five small early-18th-century shrines with sculptures depicting the Stations of the Cross, a testament to the devotion of the local population.

Antigos Paços do Concelho (Old Council Chamber)

The old council chamber, dating from the 14th century, but remodelled at the beginning of the 17th century, has a painted wooden ceiling, and is above the arches between Praça de Santiago and the Largo da Oliveira. It now houses the Museu de Arte Primitiva Moderna – a museum of naïve art of varying quality.

ⓐ Largo da Oliveira ⓣ 253 414 186 ⓛ 09.00–12.30, 14.00–17.30 Mon–Fri, closed Sat, Sun & public holidays

Capela de São Miguel (Chapel of St Michael)

Between the castle and the ducal palace, this small, simple Romanesque chapel was built in the early 12th century. It is thought to be where Afonso Henriques was baptised and contains the tombs of several of his knights.

ⓐ Rua de Santa Maria ❶ 253 412 273 🕒 09.30–12.30, 14.00–17.00 daily

Castelo (Castle)

After the original monastery was established on the orders of the Countess Mumadona Dias, the castle was built in the 10th-century, to fend off attacks by Moors and Normans, and strengthened in the 12th century and enlarged in later centuries. According to tradition, King Afonso Henriques was born here. But once the castle, with its seven towers, lost its defensive purpose, it became a prison, and was then abandoned and declined until the 1940s when it was declared a National Monument and restored. After admiring the castle, climb to the top of the battlements to get a view of Guimarães and the surrounding countryside – and if you go through the small opening to get to the top of the keep (admission charge), there's an even better view.

ⓐ Rua de Santa Maria ❶ 253 412 273 🕒 09.30–12.30, 14.00–17.30 daily

Igreja de Nossa Senhora de Oliveira (Church of Our Lady of the Olive Tree)

In the heart of the old town, this church was rebuilt on the orders of João I at the end of the 14th century. The tower was

⬥ *Pick a café and watch the world go by – Largo da Oliveira*

added in 1513, and the chancel enlarged at the end of the 17th century. The chapel in the sacristy is covered in tiles. Next to the church is the Salado memorial, a Gothic monument dating from the 14th century, built to commemorate the battle of Salado in 1340.

ⓐ Largo da Oliveira ⒪ 07.15–12.00, 15.30–19.30 daily

Penha

The hill of Penha is 2 km (1 mile) to the southeast of Guimarães. You can get up the wooded slopes to the 617-m (2,020-ft) peak by car, bus (from opposite the main tourist office) or, by far the most fun option, the 10-minute cable car ride from the Parque das Hortas. Either way, you will find a campsite, a mini-golf course, walks, jogging circuits, horse riding, picnic areas and restaurants and cafés on the hill. You'll also get superb views of the surrounding area. The main sight (on the lower slopes) is the Mosteiro de Santa Marinha de Costa, founded in 1154, probably on the site of a pre-Roman temple. The monastery was originally Augustinian, but from 1528 housed monks of the Order of St Jerome. The 18th-century church has a rococo façade, with mid-19th-century alterations in the interior. The monastery was badly damaged by a fire in 1951, but was sensitively restored, and is now a *pousada* (state-run hotel), with the gardens and some areas open to the public.

Praça de Santiago (Santiago Square)

Originally medieval, the square, with its lively café terraces in good weather, is named after St James, who was supposed to have brought an image of the Virgin Mary to place in a pagan temple that once stood in the square, where most of the houses are 17th century.

ⓐ Praça de Santiago

CULTURE

Centro Cultural Vila Flor (Vila Flor Cultural Centre)

This modern centre – near the railway station and on the way to the old town – opened in 2005 in the grounds of a 17th-century mansion, as part of the city's attempts to prepare for the 2012 European Capital of Culture nomination. It has exhibition spaces, parking, two state-of-the-art auditoriums, and is now the base for the Jazz Festival. It also has a lively and stylish café, on the lower level (🕒 until 02.00 on most days, 04.00 during the Jazz Festival). The old Vila Flor houses temporary art exhibitions. There are performances, exhibitions and events throughout the year, and it's well worth checking out what's on. The terraced gardens are also very appealing.

ⓐ Avenida D Afonso Henriques 701 ☎ 253 424 700
ⓦ www.aoficina.pt 🕒 Vary according to events, but 08.00–12.00, 14.00–16.00 daily for gardens. Admission charge for events and exhibitions

Museu Arqueológico Martins Sarmento (Martins Sarmento Archaeological Museum)

Outside the old town, near Largo do Toural, the city's main square, this archaeological museum is housed in an 18th–19th-century mansion with a splendid garden, once owned by the archaeologist after whom it was named. The expertly

displayed exhibits are of the pre-Roman culture of the area.
🅐 Rua Paio Galvão ☎ 253 478 952 🕙 09.30–12.30, 14.00–18.00
Tues–Sun, closed Mon & public holidays. Admission charge

Museu de Alberto Sampaio (Alberto Sampaio Museum)

This museum – occupying an old priory, chapter house and
cloister – was created in 1928 on the site of the monastery
Guimarães originally grew up around. It houses the treasures of
the local churches. Some of the exhibits go back to medieval
times, and there is a fine collection of silverware. For a museum
of mostly religious artefacts, it is remarkably interesting and the
high-quality exhibits are well displayed.
🅐 Rua Alfredo Guimarães ☎ 253 423 910 🕙 10.00–18.00
Tues–Sun, closed Mon & public holidays. Admission charge (free
Sun mornings)

Paço dos Duques (Ducal Palace)

This massive palace was built in the 15th century, for Afonso,
later Duke of Bragança, illegitimate son of King João I. The
architecture is unusual for Portugal – its steep roofs and
cylindrical chimneys are more reminiscent of northern Europe –
the architect was probably French. The palace went into serious
decline from the 16th century, and was near ruin by the 20th
century, but was rebuilt between 1937 and 1959, and then
became a museum. Attracting 300,000 visitors a year, it is now
the third-most-visited attraction in Portugal, as well as being
the president's official northern residence. The collection
consists of tapestries, furniture, porcelain and other decorative
art from the 17th and 18th centuries, as well as arms and armour

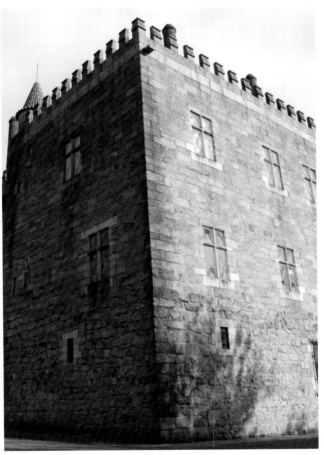

The imposing form of the Paço dos Duques (Ducal Palace)

from the 15th and 16th centuries. Concerts and other events are also held here. The Renaissance fountain in Largo Martins Sarmento, near the palace, was built in 1583, and originally stood in Toural, the city's main square.

ⓐ Rua de Santa Maria ⓣ 253 412 273 ⓛ 09.30–12.30, 14.00–17.30 daily. Admission charge (free Sun morning)

RETAIL THERAPY

There aren't a huge number of shopping opportunities in the old town, but there are a couple of good craft shops, selling pottery, embroidery and wooden objects:

Art'iago ⓐ Praça de Santiago ⓣ 253 415 795 ⓛ varies seasonally
Prometeu ⓐ Rua de Santa Maria ⓣ 253 512 640 ⓛ varies seasonally

TAKING A BREAK

Cinecitta £ Under the arches (good if it rains), with tables outside in the square as well, a snack bar with movie posters on the walls. You can get salads, sandwiches, soups and ice cream.
ⓐ Praça de Santiago ⓣ 96 379 6910 ⓛ 08.00–24.00 Tues–Sun, Sat–Wed 08.00–02.00

Cozhinha Regional Santiago £–££ A comforting place serving good fish, veal, sausages and daily specials. Tables outside in good weather. ⓐ Praça de Santiago 16–17 ⓣ 253 516 669
ⓛ 12.00–15.00, 19.00–22.00 Mon–Sat, closed Sun

El Rei £–££ Well located, and considered by many to be the best restaurant in the old town. ⓐ Praça de Santiago 20 ⓣ 253 419 096 ⓛ 13.00–15.00, 19.30–22.00 Mon–Sat, closed Sun

Solar do Arco ££ A local favourite, serving local cuisine and daily specials. ⓐ Rua de Santa Maria 50 ⓣ 253 513 072 ⓛ 12.00–15.00, 19.00–22.00 daily, closed Sun in Jan

ACCOMMODATION

Guimarães Youth Hostel £ The budget option in town, the Youth Hostel has accommodation options ranging from a self-catering apartment to double bedrooms and dorms, plus the usual kitchen and bar. Disabled access. ⓐ Complexo Multifuncional de Couros – Largo do Cidade ⓣ 253 421 380
ⓦ www.pousadasjuventude.pt

Hotel Ibis Guimarães ££ With 67 comfortable rooms, the Ibis offers a good value and reliable choice in the centre of town. ⓐ Avenida Conde Margaride 12, Creixomil ⓣ 253 424 900
ⓦ www.ibis.com

Pousada da Oliveira ££ With a very good restaurant, in a row of 16th-century houses. Both comfortable and tastefully decorated. ⓐ Rua de Santa Maria ⓣ 253 514 157 ⓦ www.pousadas.pt

Braga

Braga has been one of the main centres of Catholicism in Portugal since its development in the late 11th century under its first bishop. Founded as the Roman settlement of Bracara Augusta (probably of earlier Celtic origin), the town grew around its cathedral, and was eventually walled. It remained a devout backwater until the 16th century, when the bishop Diogo de Sousa developed it further, and fine Renaissance architecture was added. The historic town centre remained largely unchanged until the 19th century, apart from a flourish of baroque buildings a century earlier. Many of the greatest changes took place only after the Revolution of 1974, so that Braga is now the third largest city in Portugal, with a population of 150,000, plus thousands of university students. It is a centre of the textile industry. The centre, which was seriously deteriorating, was comprehensively restored from the 1980s onwards. Braga's reputation as a pretty conservative place is offset by the student population, which ensures that it's far livelier these days. The city also has an impressive football stadium, built (one side is against a cliff) for Euro 2004. Indeed, in the words of one resident, the main activities of Braga today are 'praying, shopping and construction'. The most important festivals are São João in June, Bom Jesus (at Whitsun) and Semana Santa (Holy Week, before Easter) – all of them lively and colourful.

GETTING THERE

Braga is 53 km (33 miles) northeast of Porto. You can get there by train from S Bento or Campanhã stations in only an hour (the best and most reliable option), or you can drive or take a Renex bus, both of which will take over an hour. From Guimarães, it's only a 30-minute drive or 45-minute bus ride to Braga, and well worth combining the two for a day trip. The bus station is a short walk to the west of the town centre, and the spanking new railway station (which retains the exterior of the old, blue-tiled one) a slightly longer walk to the south. There are several car parks, a number of them underground.

Tourist office ⓐ Avenida da Liberdade 1 ⓣ 253 262 550 ⓦ www.cm-braga.pt ⓛ 09.00–20.00 Mon–Fri, 09.00–12.30, 14.00–19.00 Sat & Sun, June–Sept; 09.00–12.30, 14.00–18.30 Mon–Fri, 09.00–12.30, 14.00–17.30 Sat & Sun, Oct–May

SIGHTS & ATTRACTIONS

There aren't that many formal sights in Braga, and you'll probably want to simply wander round the uplifting, surprisingly broad and mainly pedestrianised streets of the old town, the large and lively main square, Praça da Republica, with its fountains and cafés, and the shops of the soon to be pedestrianised Avenida de Liberdade which comes off it. Down the avenue, have a look at the old theatre (Theatro Circo), sumptuously restored inside: it reopened in 2006 after a closure of seven years. The tower you see behind the Praça da Republica is the Torre de Menagem, the keep of a castle built in 1738. The old town is just south of the Praça da Republica. The first street to head for in the old town should be Rua do Souto. Note, as you walk around, that many of the shops sell religious objects. At the café called Frigideiras do Cantinho (ⓐ Largo S João do

Souto, 1) on your walk, check out the Roman remains below the glass floor. If you have time, also try to get to Bom Jesus (see below). You should be able to see the best of Braga and Bom Jesus in little more than half a day.

Antigo Paço Arquiepiscopal (Old Bishop's Palace)

The massive old bishop's palace, near the cathedral, consists of three buildings dating from different periods. The east wing, facing the attractive Santa Bárbara gardens, is 16th century but in the Gothic style; the west wing is late-18th-century baroque, and the south part of the edifice is a mixture of styles from the 16th to 18th centuries. The building now houses the municipal library, as well as being part of the University of Minho. Admire the fine reading room with its coffered ceiling.

ⓐ Rua de Misericórdia or Largo do Paço ⓣ 253 601 187
ⓛ 09.00–12.00, 14.00–20.00 Mon–Fri, closed Sat, Sun & public holidays

Bom Jesus do Monte

Try not to miss this church and its esplanade, a major attraction of the region, and one of the most famous buildings in Portugal. It's on the top of a hill 5 km (3 miles) east of the city centre, and you can get there on foot, climbing the 800 steps (with 19 chapels on the way up) of the magnificent stairway as pilgrims do. Or go by bus and foot (take the No 2 from Av de Liberdade), or get to the top by a water-powered late-19th-century funicular, which climbs 115m (381ft). Otherwise you can drive or take a (reasonably priced) taxi. When you get to the top of the hill, with its panoramic views, you will find the amazing baroque

⬤ *The church of Bom Jesus do Monte, one of the most famous in Portugal*

church commissioned by archbishop Maura-Teles in 1723, completed 60 years later, with a double staircase leading up to it – a local favourite for weddings. Bom Jesus more or less turns into a resort area in summer and at weekends, with people bringing picnics to eat in the gardens, eating at the hotels and cafés by the church, or taking part in the various activities available.

Church: ☎ 253 676 636 🕐 08.30–18.30 daily May–Sept, 08.30–17.30 daily Oct–Apr

CULTURE

Museu da Imagem (Photographic Museum)

Braga's photographic museum, opened in 1999, is in an old deep-pink house, just by the Arca da Porta Nova, the city gate dating from 1772. Check the tourist office website for details of the latest exhibitions.

ⓐ Campo dos Hortas 35–37 ☎ 253 278 633 🕐 11.00–19.00 Tues–Fri, 14.30–18.00 Sat & Sun, closed Mon. Admission charge

Palácio dos Biscaínhos (Biscaínhos Palace)

An 18th-century baroque palace, with fine gardens, which has a collection of decorative arts, redolent of the lifestyles of 17th- and 18th-century aristocrats, and completely in keeping with the building. ⓐ Rua dos Biscaínhos ☎ 253 217 645 🕐 10.00–12.15, 14.00–17.30 Tues–Sun, closed Mon. Admission charge

The Museu da Imagem (Photographic Museum)

Sé Catedral (Cathedral)

The magnificent cathedral is the oldest in Portugal, consecrated in 1093 on the site of a Moorish mosque. The building is essentially Romanesque and Gothic, with baroque alterations. There are several chapels, and you will see many people praying at shrines. Note the two baroque organs and the tiles in the main chapel, and also try to visit the treasury upstairs (guided tour only), one of the richest in Portugal, and the Capela dos Reis (Kings' Chapel) with its Gothic vaulted roof.
ⓐ Rua D Paio Mendes ⓣ 253 263 317 ⓛ Church: 07.45–19.00 daily Apr–Sept, 07.45–18.30 daily Oct–Mar; Treasury: 08.30–17.30 daily. Admission charge for Treasury

RETAIL THERAPY

You'll find several craft, clothes and shoe shops in the old town, as well as chain, designer and international shops in the Avenida de Liberdade.

TAKING A BREAK

A Brasileira £ A blue-tiled exterior in this old-fashioned but charming café, which is a local institution. ⓐ Largo Barão de São Marinha ⓣ 253 262 104

Café Astoria £ One of the city's best (and oldest) cafés, with good snacks and an attractive atmosphere. ⓐ Praça de Republica ⓣ 253 273 944 ⓛ Open late Fri & Sat, closed Sun

⬥ *Praça da Republica, the large and lively main square of Braga*

Café Vianna £ Great snacks in this fashionable art nouveau place. ⓐ Praça de Republica ① 253 262 336 ② 08.00–02.00 daily

Abade de Priscos £–££ A reliable restaurant serving Portuguese specialities. ⓐ Praça Mouzinho de Albuquerque 7 ① 253 276 650 ② closed Sun & Mon

Brito's £–££ Good traditional food and local wine, in a friendly setting. ⓐ Praça Mouzinho de Albuquerque 49 ① 253 617 576 ② closed Wed

Inácio ££ High-quality local cooking in a traditional atmosphere. ⓐ Campo das Hortas, 4 ① 253 613 3 25 ② closed Tues

● *Porto's antiquated trams are an attraction in themselves*

PRACTICAL
information

Directory

GETTING THERE

By air

Porto's international airport is Francisco Sá Carneiro. There are few direct flights from the UK: the best choice is Portugal's main carrier, TAP Air Portugal (twice daily from Heathrow, once daily from Gatwick). Flight time is just over two hours. Fares can be very reasonable if you book well in advance. Ryanair flies from Stansted.
TAP Air Portugal ❶ reservations: 0845 601 0932 Ⓦ www.flytap.com
Ryanair Ⓦ www.ryanair.com

Many people are aware that air travel emits CO_2, which contributes to climate change. You may be interested in the possibility of lessening the environmental impact of your flight through the charity Climate Care, which offsets your CO_2 by funding environmental projects around the world. Visit
Ⓦ www.climatecare.org

By train

You can get to Porto's Campanhã station by train from the UK via Eurostar to Paris, onward through France via Bordeaux, and then through Spain and northern Portugal, changing trains at least twice more – a long and complex journey that will probably be more expensive than flying.
Rail Europe ❶ 08705 848 848 Ⓦ www.raileurope.co.uk
CP (Portuguese Railways) Ⓦ www.cp.pt

By car

You'll need at least one overnight stop if you drive from the UK to Porto (via France and Spain), crossing the Channel to France by Eurotunnel or ferry; but, if you don't want such a long drive, take a ferry overnight to northern Spain (Santander or Bilbao). It will still take the best part of a day to drive to Porto, and costs can be high.

Eurotunnel ⓣ 08705 35 35 35 ⓦ www.eurotunnel.com

Brittany Ferries ⓦ www.brittany-ferries.com

P&O Ferries ⓦ www.poferries.com

ACP (Portuguese Automobile Club) for emergency assistance ⓣ 228 340 001

Route planner ⓦ www.rac.co.uk

TRAVEL INSURANCE

Visitors from the UK are covered by EU reciprocal health schemes while in Portugal; you will need a European Health Insurance Card (EHIC). This guarantees emergency treatment only. Always make sure you have adequate travel insurance, covering not only health, but possessions, etc. All non-EU travellers should make sure they have adequate insurance before they travel.

ENTRY FORMALITIES

Documentation

Passports are needed by UK visitors and all others, except EU citizens who can produce a national identity card. EU (including UK) citizens do not require a visa. US, Canadian, Australian and New Zealand visitors do not require a visa for visits of up to three months. Other travellers should check in their own country about visa requirements. ⓦ www.eurovisa.info

Customs

Residents of the UK, Ireland and other EU countries may bring into Portugal personal possessions and goods for personal use, including a reasonable amount of tobacco and alcohol, provided they have been bought in the EU. There are few formalities at the points of entry into Portugal. Residents of non-EU countries, and EU residents arriving from a non-EU country, may bring in up to 400 cigarettes and 50 cigars or 50 g (2 oz) tobacco; 2 litres (3 bottles) of wine; and 1 litre (approx. 2 pints) of spirits and liqueurs.

MONEY

The euro (€) (€1 = 100 cents) comes in notes of €5, €10, €20, €50, €100, €200 and €500, and coins of €1 and €2 and 1, 2, 5, 10, 20 and 50 cents.

ATM machines (*Multibanco*) can be found at the airport, and are widely available around Porto. They accept most debit and credit cards. They are the quickest and most convenient way (and often the cheapest) to obtain cash. Instructions are normally available in English.

Credit cards (especially Visa and MasterCard) are generally accepted except at smaller shops, in simple restaurants and at markets. There are plenty of banks and bureaux de change.

HEALTH, SAFETY & CRIME

It is safe to drink tap water, as most people do, although many prefer to drink mineral water, which is cheap. There are no major precautions you need to take when eating local food – except being careful about seafood, and in simpler places which might seem unhygienic to you. So it would be sensible to take over-the-counter drugs for an upset stomach. But, on the whole, you need worry no more than at home.

Medical care in Portugal is of a decent standard, but expensive unless you have suitable travel insurance. Most minor ailments can be dealt with at pharmacies (*farmácia*), indicated by green cross signs, where qualified staff offer medical advice and dispense a wide range of medicines.

Porto is generally safe, but you should be careful late at night, in the alleys near the river, in the Ribeira district for instance, and in or near the railway station. Otherwise, take the usual sensible precautions against pickpockets and bag-snatchers, such as keeping your bag or camera close to you. You might also be approached by beggars, who you should ignore.

In general, the police try to be helpful, but might well not speak English, and can be somewhat authoritarian: try not to argue. The three types of police you might come across are: municipal police (Polícia Municipal) are unarmed and largely deal with traffic; PSP (Polícia de Segurança Pública) wear blue uniforms and deal with crime and lost property; GNR (Guarda Nacional Republicana) wear blue-grey uniforms and operate in country districts and on motorways.

If you are robbed, you should make a statement (*formulário de participação de roubo*) at your nearest police station to help when making an insurance claim.

See also Emergencies (page 138).

OPENING HOURS

Some shops are open 09.00 or 10.00 to 18.00 or 19.00 Monday to Saturday, though others take a lunchtime break, and normally open 09.00–13.00, 15.00–19.00. Many shops are closed on Saturday afternoon. Large supermarkets and shopping centres open seven days a week. The covered Bolhão market in Porto is open 08.00–17.00 Mon–Fri, 08.00–13.00 Sat.

Offices usually open 09.00–13.00, 15.00–17.00 Monday to Friday; banks open 08.30–15.00 Monday to Friday. All are closed on public holidays.

Museums, galleries and monuments normally open 10.00–12.30, 14.00–18.00, although some don't close for lunch. Many also close on public holidays, and almost all on Monday or Wednesday (if they are palaces). Some churches close for a couple of hours during the day; others are kept locked and you will have to approach the caretaker to be let in.

Pharmacies are open 09.00–13.00, 15.00–19.00 Monday to Saturday (some closing Saturday afternoon, others opening Sunday). A list of late or 24-hour pharmacies is on the door or window of those which keep regular hours.

TOILETS

Public toilets aren't particularly widespread, though you will find them at the railway station, and there are coin-operated cubicles in some of Porto's main squares. The best bet is to use those at shopping centres, museums and monuments, which tend to be well kept. Otherwise, having a drink at one of the smarter hotels or cafés is also a good option. But beware of simpler bars and eating places, where facilities might easily be insalubrious.

CHILDREN

The Portuguese, like most southern Europeans, are highly welcoming towards children. The majority of hotels will normally be very helpful if you are travelling with small children, and most restaurants will gladly serve them. Remember though that servings are large, so ask for a *meia dose* (half-portion).

Sun protection will be required only in the summer. Insect bites, however, might be a problem, and you could bring sting-relief and other items with you – or you will find them on sale in pharmacies.

Special infant needs, such as baby food and nappies, are widely available from supermarkets and other outlets, but for a shorter stay it is easier to bring familiar brands from home. Don't expect much in the way of nappy-changing facilities.

🔺 *A Ribeira* farmacia *(pharmacy)*

Infants (under 5) are allowed in free to museums and other attractions, and under-12s pay half price. The same applies to trains, but not the metro, trams and buses – where you will have to pay full fare for them.

Unfortunately very few of the attractions mentioned in this book will appeal to young children, but a trip up the Douro might be attractive, as might a tram ride (and the tram museum), the area at the mouth of the Douro, or a visit to the Parque de Serralves or the Parque da Cidade (see pages 93 and 94). The garden of Palácio de Cristal (see page 93) has a children's play area, and a building (by the play area) with various computer activities for kids.

COMMUNICATIONS
Public phones

Porto telephone numbers start with 22, followed by seven digits. When calling from anywhere in Portugal (including Porto), dial all nine digits. To call Porto from outside Portugal, dial the international prefix (00) followed by 351 (the country code for Portugal), then the nine digit number. Calling from Portugal to abroad: dial 00, followed by the country code (UK 44, Republic of Ireland 353, USA and Canada 1, Australia 61, New Zealand 64, South Africa 27), the area code (leaving out the first 0 if there is one) and the number.

Card- and (rarer) coin-operated public phone booths are widely available. Some of Porto's phone booths are based on the old red British type. You can buy phone cards (*cartões telefónicos*) at newsagents, tobacconists, post offices and kiosks – cards come at various prices; PIN-activated cards are cheaper for long distance and international calls; some phones accept credit cards. The cheapest time for calls is 21.00–09.00 Mon–Fri, and all day at weekends and on public holidays.

Incidentally, if you buy a Passe Porto (Porto Card) at a tourist office (see page 137), it will come with a free phone card with €1.50 credit.

Useful numbers Local directory enquiries 118; International directory enquiries 177; International operator 171 (reverse charge calls); Freephone numbers start with 800; Portuguese mobile numbers start with 9

Mobile phones

Porto has good mobile phone coverage, but check with your service provider before you leave home which local service you should use to get the best rates.

Post

Post offices (marked CCT) can be found throughout Porto. The main office (ⓐ Praça General Humberto Delgado ① 223 400 200) is open ① 08.00–21.00 Mon–Fri, 09.00–18.00 Sat, 09.00–12.30, 14.00–18.00 Sun; smaller offices open ① 09.00–18.00 Mon–Fri. All post offices are closed on public holidays. You can buy stamps (*selos*) at post offices or at tobacconists. Postcards to the UK and Ireland take around a week, somewhat longer to non-European destinations. Regular postboxes are red (the blue ones are for special deliveries and airmail) and resemble those found in Britain.

Current rates for sending postcards are Europe €0.56, North America, Australia and New Zealand €0.72.

Internet

Internet access is widespread in Porto, with internet cafés and connections fairly easy to find, including at bigger post offices and in libraries, and all the larger or smarter hotels provide internet connections. Wi-fi coverage is also good. Check for your nearest internet point with your hotel or the local tourist office. Expect to pay around €2–€3 per hour.

ELECTRICITY

Portugal runs on 220 V with two-pin plugs. British appliances will need a simple adaptor, best obtained in most UK electrical shops, or at the Eurostar station or the airport you leave from. You might have difficulty finding adaptors in Porto. US and other equipment designed for 110 V will normally need a transformer.

TRAVELLERS WITH DISABILITIES

Portugal isn't generally well adapted to the needs of travellers with disabilities, and Porto's steep hills and cobbled streets aren't particularly easy to navigate. There are good facilities for those with disabilities at the airport, in some museums, and the more modern hotels, as well as many metro stations (some have lifts) and on newer local trains. But otherwise, although things are improving all the time, you might find it difficult. Check with the tourist office (see page 137).

Secretariado Nacional Para a Reabiltação e Integração des Pessoas com Deficiência National government organisation providing information about accessibility. ⓐ Av Conde de Valbom 63, Lisbon ❶ 217 929 500 ⓦ www.snripd.mts.gov.pt

RADAR The principal UK forum and pressure group for people with disabilities. ⓐ 12 City Forum, 250 City Road, London EC1V 8AF ⓣ 020 7250 3222 ⓦ www.radar.org.uk

SATH (Society for Accessible Travel & Hospitality) advises US-based travellers with disabilities. ⓐ 347 Fifth Ave, Suite 610, New York, NY 10016 ⓣ 212 447 7284 ⓦ www.sath.org

FURTHER INFORMATION

There are three tourist offices (*Turismo*) in the middle of Porto:

The main city one: ⓐ Rua Clube des Fenianos 25 ⓣ 223 393 470 ⓦ www.portoturismo.pt ⓛ 09.00–17.30 Mon–Fri, 09.30–16.30 Sat, Sun & public holidays

In the UNESCO World Heritage area: ⓐ Rua do Infante D Henrique 63 ⓣ 222 060 412/413 ⓦ www.portoturismo.pt ⓛ 09.00–17.30 Mon–Fri, 09.30–16.30 Sat, Sun & public holidays

The state tourist office (ITP): ⓐ Praça Dom Joàn I 43 ⓣ 222 057 514 ⓛ 09.00–19.30 Mon–Fri, 09.30–15.30 Sat, Sun & public holidays.

Portuguese national tourist website ⓦ www.visitportugal.com

Regional website ⓦ www.visitportoandnorth.com

Online directory ⓦ www.portugalvirtual.pt, with much useful information

Emergencies

For all emergency services (national number) – 112

MEDICAL SERVICES
The main hospitals are:

Hospital Geral de Santo António Some English-speaking doctors. ⓐ Largo Prof Abel Salazar ⓣ 222 077 500
Hospital Escolar São João To the north of the city. ⓐ Alameda Prof Hernani Monteiro ⓣ 225 512 100

Ask your hotel, the British consulate or the tourist office for a list of English-speaking doctors and dentists near where you are staying.

POLICE
The main stations are:

Policia de Turismo (Tourist Police) English spoken, near the main tourist office, and the place to go, if you can. ⓐ Rua Clube dos Fenianos 11 ⓣ 222 081 833 ⓛ 08.00–02.00 daily
Policia de Segurança Pública ⓐ Rua Augousto Rosa ⓣ 222 087 848
Policia Municipal ⓐ Bairro Rainha D Leonor ⓣ 226 198 260

EMBASSIES & CONSULATES
Australian Embassy ⓐ 2nd floor, Avenida da Liberdade 200, 1250-147 Lisbon ⓣ 213 101 500

Canadian Embassy ⓐ 3rd floor, Avenida da Liberdade 196, 1269-121 Lisbon ① 213 164 600

Irish Embassy ⓐ Rua da Imprensa a Estrela 1–4, 1200-684 Lisbon ① 213 929 440

South African Consulate Rua António José Da Costa 78, 4150-090 Porto ① 226 076 010 🕒 09.00–12.00 Mon–Fri, closed Sat & Sun

UK Consulate ⓐ Travessa Barão de Forrester 86, 4400-034 Porto (Vila Nova de Gaia) ① 226 184 789 🕒 09.30–12.30, 14.30–16.00 Mon–Fri, closed Sat & Sun

US Consulate ⓐ Avenida da Boavista 3523, 4100-139 Porto ① 226 186 607 🕒 08.00–12.00, 13.00–17.00 Mon–Fri, closed Sat & Sun

---

EMERGENCY PHRASES

Help! Socorro! *Sookohrroo!*   **Fire!** Fogo! *Fohgoo!*

Stop! Pare! *Pahreh!*

Call an ambulance/a doctor/the police/the fire brigade!

Chame uma ambulância/um médico/a polícia/os bombeiros!

*Shami ooma angboolangsya/oong medeekoo/
a pooleesseeya/oosh bombehroosh!*

SPOT A CITY IN SECONDS

This great range of pocket city guides will have you in the know in no time. Lightweight and packed with detail on the most important things from shopping and sights to non-stop nightlife, they knock spots off chunkier, clunkier versions. Titles include:

Amsterdam	Bratislava	Glasgow	Madrid	Salzburg
Antwerp	Bruges	Gothenburg	Marrakech	Sarajevo
Athens	Brussels	Granada	Milan	Seville
Barcelona	Bucharest	Hamburg	Monte Carlo	Sofia
Belfast	Budapest	Hanover	Munich	Stockholm
Belgrade	Cardiff	Helsinki	Naples	Strasbourg
Berlin	Cologne	Hong Kong	New York	St Petersburg
Bilbao	Copenhagen	Istanbul	Nice	Tallinn
Bologna	Cork	Kiev	Oslo	Turin
	Dubai	Krakow	Palermo	Valencia
	Dublin	Leipzig	Palma	Venice
	Dubrovnik	Lille	Paris	Verona
	Dusseldorf	Lisbon	Prague	Vienna
	Edinburgh	Ljubljana	Porto	Vilnius
	Florence	London	Reykjavik	Warsaw
	Frankfurt	Lyon	Riga	Zagreb
	Gdansk		Rome	Zurich
	Geneva			
	Genoa			

CITY SPOTS **HAMBURG**

CITY SPOTS **VILNIUS**

CITY SPOTS **BILBAO**

CITY SPOTS **NEW YORK**

CITY SPOTS **GLASGOW**

Available from all good bookshops, your local Thomas Cook travel store or browse and buy on-line at www.thomascookpublishing.com

Thomas Cook
Publishing

Thomas Cook

The publishers would like to thank the following individuals and organisations for providing their copyright photos for this book: Anwer Bati: all photographs except: p32 © Jordi Cubells Biela – FOTOLIA; p42–3 © TAOLMOR - FOTOLIA.

Copy editor: Lynn Bresler
Proofreader: Ian Faulkner

Send your thoughts to
books@thomascook.com

- **Found a great bar, club, shop or must-see sight that we don't feature?**

- **Like to tip us off about any information that needs updating?**

- **Want to tell us what you love about this handy little guidebook and more importantly how we can make it even handier?**

Then here's your chance to tell all! Send us ideas, discoveries and recommendations today and then look out for your valuable input in the next edition of this title. As an extra 'thank you' from Thomas Cook Publishing, you'll be automatically entered into our exciting prize draw.

Send an email to the above address (stating the book's title) or write to: CitySpots Project Editor, Thomas Cook Publishing, PO Box 227, The Thomas Cook Business Park, Unit 18, Coningsby Road, Peterborough PE3 8SB, UK.